AR
CAD
IA

CHATSWORTH, ARCADIA, NOW

SEVEN SCENES FROM THE LIFE OF AN ENGLISH COUNTRY HOUSE

John-Paul Stonard

Foreword by
The Duke & Duchess of Devonshire

Photographs by
Victoria Hely-Hutchinson

Rizzoli Electa

FOREWORD

THE DUKE & DUCHESS OF DEVONSHIRE

We are the sixteenth generation of the Cavendish family to have lived at Chatsworth, and many of our forebears have left their mark on the place. In 1549, Bess of Hardwick selected the site overlooking the River Derwent for her house, which provides the footprint of today's Chatsworth. The first Duke replaced the original Elizabethan building with a completely modern house, to reflect his power and wealth in a country which had just undergone the 'Glorious Revolution' of 1688. The sixth Duke's nineteenth-century additions revolved around his Great Dining Room, Sculpture Gallery and Ballroom.

As the current custodians of Chatsworth, our preoccupations have been more practical than those of some of our predecessors. This book marks the completion of the major refurbishment programme—known at Chatsworth as 'the Masterplan'—during which the house was encased in scaffolding, the grime from three centuries' exposure to the Derbyshire elements was removed from its stone façade, and window frames on the South and West Fronts were re-gilded. These building works—the majority of them hidden from sight—were necessary from a physical point of view, so that the fabric and services in most parts of the house are now in better condition than for a very long time.

The work also marked the final part of a gradual alteration in the use and purpose of the house, a change that started after the Second World War, when my parents came to realize that Chatsworth's future lay more as a tourist destination than as a private house occasionally open to visitors. Notably, the visitor route and facilities have been greatly improved—including, at long last, enhanced access for those with restricted mobility, through the installation of a new lift serving all floors of the house.

We lived at Chatsworth throughout the Masterplan, using different rooms as the work progressed. For two years our bedroom was in the attics; there are eighty-two steps from the ground floor to the top, so it was better not to leave your spectacles upstairs in the morning. With every change we made new discoveries about the house, including the number of huge voids between floors, big enough to walk in, and the Elizabethan partitions on the north side second floor. It was 'interesting', but well worth any inconvenience —we could see progress on a daily basis, we were able to make on-the-spot decisions, and we learned from the myriad craftspeople, enjoying privileged up-close views of their work.

While this was principally a restoration project, we made a few physical alterations of our own, such as a new shower room, a room for our secretaries where the Billiard Room had been, and a new entrance to our drawing room. There were also a few permanent physical additions, such as the masons' marks on the east elevation of the Inner Court and three site-specific ceramic installations, most importantly in the North Sketch Gallery.

There is one thing that hasn't changed—one constant—which is that the craftsmen and women who have worked on the various iterations of the building since the mid-sixteenth century have all been exceptionally gifted. The construction of the first Duke's Baroque house and the sixth Duke's Victorian wing is of incredible quality. The only significant thing we had to do, apart from the stonework restoration, was to mend the foundations; these had been eroded by a constant flow of water for nearly three hundred years, from where we are not sure. This high standard was maintained throughout the refurbishments. The changes have been many, mostly in themselves quite minor, but taken together they have made a mark.

As the Masterplan came to an end, we invited John-Paul Stonard to tell the story of Chatsworth, which he has done through a series of essays, seven 'Arcadian' scenes that travel backwards to the origins of the house. Meanwhile, Victoria Hely-Hutchinson's photographs show the house as it was in 2019–20, and offer fresh glimpses of artefacts we know well and not so well, including some which, due to their fragility, cannot often be displayed to visitors.
The book is structured in reverse chronological order, to give the sense of digging down through the sedimentary layers of history, starting today and finishing nearly five hundred years ago with the recently unearthed remnants of Bess of Hardwick's building.

The overriding impression of living at Chatsworth is one of peace. The house is entirely benign, the views are wonderfully calm, and a sense of optimism prevails. We are constantly reminded of the many layers of time and history, which sometimes reveal themselves quite unpredictably. During the long drought of 2018, as the South Lawn gradually turned brown, the outline of the first Duke's parterre, beneath the windows of the State Rooms he built in anticipation of a royal visit which did not materialize, reappeared in ghostly form. Not only did this demonstrate the accuracy of Jan Siberechts' painting of the house and grounds in 1703; it was also a startling reminder that the past has a tendency to rear its head when you least expect it.

PROLOGUE

ARRIVING IN ARCADIA

Let us say that you have never been to Chatsworth, but know something of the house and its history. It may stand in your mind as a sort of Arcadia: a grand palace nestled in rolling green hills, folded into its surroundings, the garden and grounds spreading out into the wider landscape.

Now let us imagine that you have actually arrived in this place, passing through the wooden doors into the North Entrance Hall, warmed by a blazing fire, then mounting the stone steps, pausing only briefly to admire the antique statues as you turn a corner. Suddenly you stop, your attention caught by the sound of footsteps that seem to come from nowhere, as a figure in a dark gown and white collar strides past. It is THOMAS HOBBES, the seventeenth-century philosopher, a wry smile playing on his lips—and in his train comes a young man with dark hair, WILLIAM CAVENDISH, the future second Earl of Devonshire, hurrying along deep in thought.

Turning the corner, you are greeted by a stranger sight still: in the middle of the Painted Hall stand two figures, one in a long green robe, pointing out images on the ceiling. It is WILLIAM CAVENDISH, the first Duke of Devonshire, and the painter LOUIS LAGUERRE: the latter is having his work explained to him by the Duke in French, his demeanour all agreement. Quickly, so as not to be noticed, you climb the stairs, two at a time, then suddenly flatten yourself against the wall as the eighth Duke SPENCER COMPTON CAVENDISH descends, elegant in white tie, shouting up to his valet who hurries after him carrying a heavy valise. From the stairwell below, the butler alerts him that his carriage is ready.

Up to a landing and a moment of repose. *Dip, dop, dip, dop*, goes the pendulum of a tall clock in the shadows, the brass mechanism stopping to whirr and release the hammer that sounds the quarter-to chime. As if on cue, opposite doors in great stone portals swing open: from one emerges the slender figure of the actor DAVID GARRICK, sporting a velvet frock coat; from the other, in sober modern dress, the artist MICHAEL CRAIG-MARTIN.

Before they can collide, they stop, skirt around each other and continue through the opposing doors, both lost and late for the same dinner.

Hurrying on to the long suite of State Rooms, you encounter all kinds of commotion: it seems that the rooms are being both created and restored at the same time. The great wood-carver SAMUEL WATSON is here with his fellow workers, LOBB and DAVIS, putting the finishing touches to a limewood festoon hanging from the cornice. A few rooms down, EVELYN CAVENDISH, the thrifty wife of the ninth Duke, is busily restoring the punched leather wall covering with the creative use of some blue paint. Absorbed in their tasks, they do not notice as you pass, though you are now brought to a halt by the sound of a loud argument: in a dark lobby, two men are almost at blows, fighting over a paintbrush. JAMES THORNHILL, his periwig slightly askew, stands amid his wall paintings showing the abduction of the Sabine women, and the young LUCIAN FREUD, who had been working next door on a more modest mural, furiously squares up to him. Best to leave them.

Moving on, you stop to catch your breath at a window and admire the view, over the lawns towards the Canal Pond. Figures flit from hedge to hedge: you glimpse an elaborate white costume, a bombardier's hat, a flash of red ribbons, and then a woman with a dazzling outfit, embroidered snakes—the Cavendish family motif—winding up the dress's shoulders. The fourth Duke, WILLIAM CAVENDISH, marches up a slope, deep in conversation with the landscape gardener LANCELOT 'CAPABILITY' BROWN. A woman riding side-saddle appears, writing in a notebook as she goes: the travel writer CELIA FIENNES. In the distance a small army of workmen dig, cart, plant—the landscape seems to change before your eyes.

Turning from the window, you make your way along corridors, down steps and around corners, then up the Oak Stairs, passing a large malachite clock, a gift from a Russian tsar, and then into the Library. Here, the librarian FRANCIS THOMPSON stoops among piles of books, intent on the arrangement he is creating. By a white marble fireplace, the second Duke, WILLIAM CAVENDISH, resplendent in the fashions of the early eighteenth century—red velvet coat flared at the hip, white cravat, breeches and stockings—is deep in conversation with a gentleman whose gold, lavishly embroidered waistcoat shows him to be very wealthy and very French: the famous connoisseur and collector PIERRE CROZAT. On the gallery above is HORACE WALPOLE, scouring the shelves with a pencil and notepad in hand, while in a far corner, wearing a tricorn hat and violet velvet frock coat, the experimental scientist HENRY CAVENDISH is checking and double-checking calculations in a white vellum notebook. The far door swings open to admit the art historian EUGENIE SELLERS STRONG, talking loudly to herself in Ancient Greek.

All this has become too much for you to take in, so you turn on your heel and enter the Great Dining Room. Every seat is occupied, the intricately modelled silver candelabras on the table gleaming new in the flickering candlelight. Among the assembled company sits the young PRINCESS VICTORIA and her mother: the girl is the centre of attention, but she remains calm and still as the activity in the ornate room whirls around her, set against the background of glowing portraits by Flemish masters. On you go still further, through a grand door to a moving spectacle: surrounded by his sculptures, the great artist ANTONIO CANOVA is deep in conversation with his patron WILLIAM CAVENDISH, the sixth Duke. Sitting to one side, LADY LOUISA EGERTON, the only daughter of the seventh Duke, is painting a watercolour of the scene. Through a side door, down a long passage… Where are you now? A telephone rings nearby, followed by the barking of dogs. DEBORAH CAVENDISH, wife of the eleventh Duke, sweeps round a corner dressed in a tweed jacket and skirt; we've just moved in, she explains, to nobody in particular, before continuing along the corridor, a wallpaper sample book in her hand.

Down more corridors, past more rooms—there are clocks everywhere, you notice, as a woman hurries past carrying a bag holding numerous keys, stopping to open the window of a tall clock; they all need winding, she says, however grand they may be. Up yet more stairs, and into the Theatre in the North Wing, to be greeted by a stirring sight indeed: two women on the stage, seemingly acting out a play. They are none other than GEORGIANA CAVENDISH, in a broad-brimmed hat decorated with an ostrich feather, and, wearing a dark gown and long strings of pearls, ELIZABETH HARDWICK herself, upright, regal, pale, magnificent. In the audience sits Elizabeth's second husband, the very first WILLIAM CAVENDISH, with whom she built the original Chatsworth; he looks up to the gallery, where Georgiana's husband, the fifth Duke, sits with his mistress, LADY ELIZABETH FOSTER.

But there's no time to waste, and there are more steps to climb, up, up, for now you are desperate for some fresh air, blue sky and a view of hills. Overwhelming! Is that not the word you hear so often used about this place? Up, finally, to the Belvedere, that lofty terrace open to the four winds. Here, at the end of your journey, are two familiar faces, STOKER and AMANDA CAVENDISH, the twelfth and current Duke and Duchess of Devonshire, hailing and beckoning you to admire the scenery. Look down, Amanda gestures, there, to that stone platform near the river, guarded by four men. On the Bower itself paces a woman with red hair and glittering finery, and a resolute, determined air: MARY, QUEEN OF SCOTS, gazing out over the river into the Derbyshire countryside.

This, then, is where you have arrived: in Arcadia.

MDCCII

MDCCII

SCENE I

ARCADIA NOW

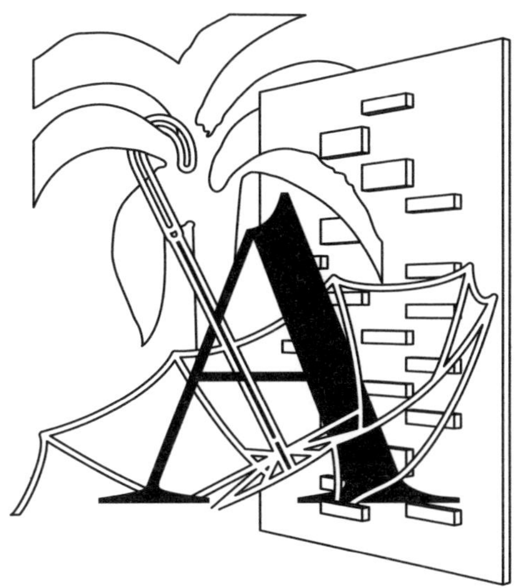

At the foot of a grassy slope by the Canal Pond, a small crowd has gathered. Oddly, ominously even, the assembled figures are holding masks against their faces, each bearing the image of a coiled snake. Behind two of these masks are STOKER and AMANDA CAVENDISH, the twelfth Duke and Duchess of Devonshire. Confronting them is a strange-looking structure painted red—a bower, strewn with large artificial flowers, shored up with red pebbles. Hushed expectancy fills the air. Suddenly, down the green bank come skipping two female figures wearing brightly coloured costumes, with thickly padded sleeves like coiled serpents. To the sounds of hypnotic, pulsating music, and the strained call of a horn fashioned from an old piece of copper plumbing, the snake women dance: now slowly, rhythmically, now frenetically, spinning and spinning around the bower. One of them lays a large artificial flower before the masked audience. The other writhes and weaves some more, and then, just as suddenly as they appeared, they flit back up over the slope. The music gradually winds to a halt and silence returns, leaving the onlookers in a state somewhere between bewilderment and wonder.

Traces of the contemporary can be found all around at Chatsworth. Unlike a museum, devoted to preserving the past, it is a living, working house, firmly embedded in the present. Even so, the past is far from absent: antiquities, sculptures old when they were acquired—from austere Roman portraits to stern Egyptian cat-gods—take their place in halls and corridors. Many of the books in the Library were considered antiquarian when they first arrived, and certainly the carved gems from Antiquity, though their colours

*Serpent carving on the façade of the first Duke's house, c.*1690s

remained fresh and rich, were very old. And yet, over the centuries, successive generations of the Cavendish family have had a near-obsessive fascination with the art and ideas of their own times. 'Almost everything was new when it landed here,' as Stoker Cavendish says, looking back over the collecting habits of his ancestors.

On that particular summer's afternoon in 2018, the Duke and Duchess were watching a performance devised by the artist Linder, titled *The Bower of Bliss,* after a scene in Edmund Spenser's long poem *The Faerie Queene.* The dazzling costumes, designed by Louise Gray, were inspired by the knotted serpent, the Cavendish family emblem—also known as the serpent 'nowed', in the arcane language of heraldry. The origin of this coiled beast is unknown, but it was present on the façade of the first Chatsworth, the house built by Elizabeth Hardwick in the 1500s, a symbol of strength and independence, writhing with contained energy. Nowadays it is found everywhere around the house, from inkwells to stair rails, and in numerous configurations on the façade, which sprung most likely from the fertile imagination of the local wood- and stone-carver Samuel Watson, and were executed with a verve that carries right through to Linder's performance in our own times. The enclosing, protective bower around which the snake women danced echoed one of the oldest structures in the grounds, in one myth said to have been built for Mary, Queen of Scots when she was imprisoned at Chatsworth by Elizabeth I—although not a shred of evidence for this exists. Like so much else at Chatsworth, with Linder's *Bower of Bliss* myths and stories from the past ripple and echo in the fresh light of the present.

The nowed serpent, twisting into the mathematical sign for infinity, is a fitting symbol for this layering of past and present at Chatsworth in the twenty-first century. Alongside old tapestries with biblical scenes you might find large abstract paintings; on the leather-lined top of a mahogany Georgian table, alongside Sèvres porcelain, stand orange-and-pink vessels, strange

Drummer, by Barry Flanagan, 1996

ceramic creations that seem to glow from within. The work of the sculptor Anthony Caro and the conceptual artist Michael Craig-Martin, as well as Linder and the American sculptor Rachel Feinstein, among countless others, have been shown inside the house and on the surrounding estate; large pieces by the likes of Barry Flanagan, Elisabeth Frink and Eilis O'Connell appear from behind bushes and across ponds; turning from a stone statue of Hercules or Athena, you are suddenly confronted by a dancing hare cast in bronze or a giant, pink, high-heeled shoe, outlined in wire.

This twenty-first century Chatsworth is largely the vision of the twelfth Duke and Duchess. They built on the work of the Duke's parents, Andrew and Deborah, who, prior to taking up residence in 1959, transformed the house into a habitable building, following almost a century in which few repairs or changes had been made and very little was added to the collections of art. Both Stoker and Amanda Cavendish were inspired by their respective parents, who bought contemporary art at a time when few others were taking the risk: the Duchess's mother, June Heywood-Lonsdale, was known for the Francis Bacon she had hanging in her dining room, just as the Duke's parents were friends of (and subjects of portraits by) Lucian Freud.

Ceramics displayed around the house express this melding of past and present. Around 1700 the first Duke displayed blue-and-white porcelain from China, and imitation porcelain from Holland, in and around fireplaces, and ranged pieces up the walls of his newly built house. Nowadays you can find a set of white porcelain vessels made by Edmund de Waal, titled *A Sounding Line*, similarly arranged, their tall, noble handmade forms standing within and around two fireplaces in the Chapel Corridor. Or giant vases by the contemporary ceramicist Felicity Aylieff, their surfaces invigorated by calligraphic sweeps of blue-and-red glaze, like free interpretations of the massive blue-and-white vases of the Chinese Kangxi Period (the sixty years after 1662) on display elsewhere in the house.

A Sounding Line (detail),
by Edmund de Waal, 2007

Or a different potter's vision: a stack of more than two hundred brightly coloured cylindrical pots, displayed in front of a bookcase holding leather-bound antiquarian volumes, diminishing in size as they stack up to the ceiling, those at the top seeming no larger than coloured clay thimbles. Here baked clay is shaped into a symbol of abundance and variety: Natasha Daintry's *Sowing Colour*, as the work is called, is based on the Fibonacci sequence of numbers, mapping patterns of natural growth.

Turn a corner and you are greeted by a stranger vision still: an entire wall covered with mysterious small blocks set into panels at varying depths in columns and rows, the colour of rich tea biscuits, light and buoyant in appearance. Some of the blocks are roughly textured, others smooth. The work is a little intimidating on first encounter, and hardly less so when you learn that you are looking at a 'DNA' portrait of the twelfth Duke and Duchess, and of their son and daughter-in-law, William and Laura, Earl and Countess of Burlington, by the artist Jacob van der Beugel.[1]

Jacob van der Beugel's *North Sketch Sequence* is unusual for a contemporary commission, filling an entire space, as did the decorative schemes created for the first Duke in the years around 1700, the sprawling ceiling paintings and carved sculptural decoration within and without. The paintings, with their allusive but flattering references to the Protestant William and Mary as King and Queen of England, were also political statements that reinforced the Duke's support for them after he helped bring about their reign following the deposition of James II. These days such works would be much harder to commission: 'If I were to build an entirely new house, with a lot of rooms,' the twelfth Duke says, 'it would be fine to do it with the architecture and the decoration—that would not be a problem. But if I want to ask an artist to produce wall or ceiling paintings that reflect the slightly left-of-centre conservative political views of this family, then that is not so easy.' Even if they are painting in a figurative, recognizable style,

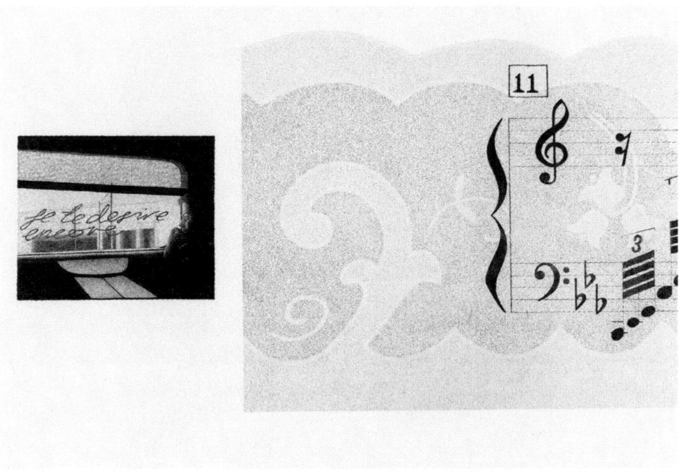

Diana and Actaeon (detail),
by Tarka Kings, 2013

artists nowadays can't use stories from myth or from the Bible in the same way, creating allegories that might reflect the views of their patron. Wall paintings tend to be abstract, responding to their architectural surrounds, signs not of political allegiance but of a broader openness to contemporary art.

Commissioned works nevertheless appear around the house that, if not political, show at least a boldness of taste and purpose. Around the dining-room table, chairs commissioned from the furniture-maker Joseph Walsh seem at first sight like strange biomorphic forms, totally unlike the Georgian mahogany seats you might otherwise expect to find. Open the door to a lavatory, and you are greeted by a set of enigmatic wall drawings by the contemporary artist Tarka Kings: they start with the story of Diana and Actaeon but then drift off, like roving thought, into images of a youth asleep on the grass, the back of a young woman's head, an automatic rifle and lines from Shelley's *Adonais*, his elegy for the poet Keats, the whole animated by a piece of music by Mozart, which starts to play after the door is opened.

What all this suggests, despite the impression of Arcadian calm, is a house constantly in motion, circling around like the nowed serpent atop the ducal coat of arms. The Devonshire Collections have both surged and diminished over time; the house itself has been built and rebuilt, rooms changing their purpose, the whole building altering its appearance within the surrounding landscape. The gilded windows and finials, glinting in the evening sunlight on the approach from the village of Edensor, could be seen in the time of the first Duke and were reinstated by the twelfth as part of a ten-year campaign of restoration. The stonework façade of the building was restored and repaired (all except the bullet holes near the north entrance from a German plane during the Second World War), with damaged stones replaced by new blocks

*View through the State Rooms, c.*1876

of Ashover Grit, a particularly dense type of sandstone, extracted from the nearby quarry of Burntwood on the Chatsworth Estate. The restoration of a water-powered turbine, a relic that survives from the earliest days of electrification (Chatsworth was the second large country house in England to have electricity installed—a good example of the Cavendish family motto 'Cavendo Tutus', or 'safety through caution'), means that the house now produces some of its own electricity, rather than relying entirely on the National Grid. As with the rebuilding of the Elizabethan house by the first Duke, what began as a modest scheme of repairs grew until it became a complete overhaul, so that much of the building, from the lead roof to the wiring and plumbing throughout, was restored or updated (to the designs and interventions of the architect Peter Inskip and the interior designer David Mlinaric). Changes to the interior meant that more works of art could be displayed: in the Old Master Drawings Cabinet, works on paper by, among others, Leonardo da Vinci, Titian, Raphael, Pieter Bruegel the Elder, Rubens, Carracci and Dürer hang under the watchful gaze of a portrait painted by Rembrandt. Other spaces around the house, notably the State Rooms and the Sculpture Gallery, have also been returned to their earliest appearances.

As a set of large rooms with a symbolic function, the State Rooms had been designed for the purpose of display. The first Duke conceived them as a royal apartment in 1690 and furnished them for the residence of the King and Queen (they were, in fact, first used by royalty only at the beginning of the twentieth century, by George V and Queen Mary, in 1913). The project to restore them to their appearance in the first Duke's time began with the scouring of old documents—eyewitness reports, building accounts—to see how they had been furnished. Objects were then reassembled, including the 'Fine old China' mentioned in an inventory of 1764, and the set of tapestries known as the *Acts of the Apostles*, copied in the 1630s from the Raphael cartoons bought some years earlier by Charles I (when Prince of Wales), and

Devonshire Hunting Tapestries hanging in the Sculpture Gallery, c.1920s

important for having been woven at Mortlake, near Richmond-upon-Thames.[2] Two elaborate mirrors made by John Gumley in 1703 were placed in the State Bedchamber and the State Closet, while Old Master paintings were hung in front of seventeenth-century Brussels tapestries. In the re-creation of these rooms, detailed research was accompanied by educated guesswork, as well as creative filling-in-the-gaps—the first Duke would undoubtedly be surprised to see any such innovations but still, hopefully, recognize his own intentions. The tall, dramatic bed in the State Bedchamber with crimson damask hangings was probably made for George I and arrived at Chatsworth only in the 1760s.[3] Walking through these rooms today, you get a strong sense of the symbolism of display, expectations rising and nerves jangling as you approach the person of the King or Queen.

The Sculpture Gallery has been restored to its appearance around 1858, the year of the death of its creator, the sixth Duke. 'It was very much Charles Noble's [Curator of Fine Arts at Chatsworth] initiative,' the present Duke says. 'He felt very strongly that it should be put back to exactly as it was, and we were delighted, because it was exactly the same guiding principle that the art adviser Jonathan Bourne instilled in us for the State Rooms.' The sculptures, almost all contemporary works bought or commissioned by the sixth Duke, had remained in position until the 1920s, when Duchess Evelyn, the wife of the ninth Duke, made changes to accommodate works of art that had arrived from Devonshire House, London, which had been sold in 1919. Four large fifteenth-century tapestries—the *Devonshire Hunting Tapestries*—would fit nowhere else but on the long walls of the Sculpture Gallery. Evelyn's passion for tapestries and textiles cast many of the sixth Duke's marbles, sculptures and their pedestals into temporary exile, some to the adjoining Orangery (by that time emptied of its trees, which had been left untended in the absence of gardeners during the First World War), some even into the cold and frequently damp surrounding garden.

Chatsworth from the South-West,
by Jonathan Warrender, 2015

Diaries and letters written by the sixth Duke, as well as his privately published *Handbook of Chatsworth and Hardwick*, were scoured for details of the original arrangement of sculptures, including the many works by Antonio Canova which he had commissioned and collected. Building accounts held in the archives were picked through for information about the arrival of the sculptures to the house (they were initially placed elsewhere, as the gallery was being built) and the positioning of wooden models—'skelliton figures of statues and vases', as the accounts record. Drawings and notes by the artist Richard Westmacott; watercolours by William Henry Hunt, and by Lady Louisa Egerton, the daughter of the seventh Duke; accounts in guidebooks, notably *The Gem of the Peak*, from 1838, by William Adam; and photographs taken later in the century—all were examined and considered in an effort to re-create the sixth Duke's vision.

Finally, stone and marble sculptures, heavy columns, two enormous giltwood tables and various vases were gathered with the assistance of heavy-lifting equipment from around the house and from the garden; sculptures were reunited with their original pedestals and the whole arranged in accordance, as far as possible, with the sixth Duke's plan.[4] 'Absolutely entirely contemporary,' Stoker Cavendish says; 'with the exception of the Alexander the Great head [a sculpture from Antiquity], everything was brand new when it arrived in the 1820s.'

To encounter these historic interiors today, alongside the sometimes baffling, often provocative forms of contemporary art, is to be reminded that what we take as 'historic' or 'antique' was once surprisingly, even shockingly new. Our story begins in the present, but then, as we continue to wander, the past gradually comes to life, like walking through an enfilade of rooms, each one taking us back fifty, one hundred, two hundred or more years. Where are we going? The hands of the clock are whirring, transporting us, back down the corridors of time…

PRESS

When this white marble bust was seen by the great German archaeologist Adolf Furtwängler in the 1890s, it had been wrongly restored to resemble a female figure, with a long tress of hair resting over one shoulder.[5] These false restorations were later removed, to reveal the head of Dionysos, recognizable from two other versions of the same sculpture that have survived as full-length figures. 'The whole attitude is one of complete repose and delightful abandon,' Furtwängler wrote of the better of these, preserved in Madrid; 'a delicious sense of enjoyment pervades the whole figure, the lines of which are rounded in the most wonderfully harmonious fashion.'

***Head of Dionysos*, late Flavian, first century AD** 16

It is the duty of the head gardener, or a member of the Garden team, to take readings from the weather station positioned on the Salisbury Lawn every day—measuring hours of sunshine, inches of rain and temperature range. These readings are recorded on slips of paper that are passed to a member of the private household, or the Duke, who notes them in the *Weather Book* kept in the Private Dining Room. Records have been kept regularly since the 1860s, completed volumes lining the walls of the Muniment Room.

Weather Book, November 2019

 Le Parc des Sources, Vichy, by David Hockney, 1970 (see page 20)

Two seated figures are admiring the view, an avenue of trees receding into the distance. Or are they looking at a painting of trees? David Hockney's first title for this work, seen here in the grand setting of the Painted Hall, was *Painting within a Painting*—it was the artifice of the landscape that he wanted to emphasize. The parkland setting in the French town of Vichy is itself artificial—the trees are planted on two sides of a triangle, giving only the effect of deep perspective recession. The seated figures are the designer Ossie Clark and the artist Peter Schlesinger, close friends of Hockney. The empty chair is for the artist himself, who has just got up to paint the scene. The combination of perspective, landscape and artifice recall a film that held a special charm for Hockney, Alain Resnais's *Last Year at Marienbad* (1961).

Le Parc des Sources, Vichy, by David Hockney, 1970

Lady Georgiana, known as 'Little G', was born in the summer of 1783 to Georgiana, Duchess of Devonshire, and her husband, the fifth Duke, after nine years of marriage. Over the fireplace in the Blue Drawing Room, Georgiana dandles her first child on her lap, playing a game of Surprise with her, the infant's arms and legs swinging joyfully in the air. Her black dress lined with white silk, and her daughter's white linen gown tied with a black sash, show that Georgiana was in mourning for her father, John Spencer, first Earl Spencer, who had died just a few months after his granddaughter's birth. The great swag of red material, antique urn and Italianate view lend a grandness to the scene, given a twist by the happy pose of mother and daughter, delighting, despite everything, in their new life together.

***Georgiana, Duchess of Devonshire, and her daughter, Georgiana*, by Joshua Reynolds, 1784**

These strange, flattened vessels, with cobalt-blue and *trompe-l'œil* decoration, contradict everything we might expect from a ceramic vessel: that it should be a rounded container, formed on the potter's wheel and painted in such a way as emphasizes the shape of the pot. Fritsch's characteristic coloured-brick patterning breaks the surfaces of the pots, making them seem transparent and boundless, as if each piece were a fragment of a larger, spectacular whole.

***Firework VII and Firework III*, by Elizabeth Fritsch, 2005, 2004**

It is the lasting image of Henry VIII—impressively broad-shouldered, white-stockinged legs apart, his mien resolute, like a wrestler decked in regal finery. In one hand he clasps a glove, which he seems on the point of throwing down, his other hand reaching for an ornate dagger hanging from his belt. The model for this portrait was painted by the German artist Hans Holbein. Once on the wall of the Privy Chamber at Whitehall Palace, it was part of a group portrait—showing Henry VIII, his father Henry VII and their wives—that was later destroyed in a fire.

Holbein's working drawing of Henry VIII for the left-hand side of the Whitehall wall painting was kept in The Devonshire Collections until the 1950s, when, in lieu of death duties, the government allocated it to the National Portrait Gallery, London. Numerous copies were made of Holbein's painted portrait, a supreme work of royal propaganda, including this version, which is attributed to the studio of the Flemish artist Hans Eworth, who was the leading portrait painter in England between the death of Holbein, in 1543, and the arrival of the Flemish painter Anthony van Dyck, in 1632. Eworth painted another version of Holbein's Henry VIII in 1567, twenty years after the King's death, which hangs at Trinity College, Cambridge. The date of the Chatsworth painting, which was made around the same time as the Trinity College portrait, has been confirmed by analysis of the wood panelling on which it was painted, suggesting oak trees felled in the eastern Baltic sometime between 1557 and 1589.

The Chatsworth portrait is recorded as having belonged to William Cavendish, first Duke of Devonshire. It hung on the stairs of his London residence at 3 St James's Square, and afterwards at Devonshire House; it was then transported to Chatsworth by the sixth Duke, who placed it in his drawing room, along with five other portraits, all in the same elaborate wide gold frames. Here Henry presides, at least for the moment, over a very different type of portrait by another German émigré painter who had moved to England: Frank Auerbach's portrait of Estella Olive West, one of the models who sat for him over a long period of years. Two studies of heads by Auerbach hang on the walls at Chatsworth. One, *E. O. W.'s Head on Her Pillow III*, was purchased by the present Duchess's mother, June Heywood-Lonsdale, shortly after it was finished in 1966—a bold acquisition at that date.

Both images of West exhibit Auerbach's characteristic thickly painted style, which could not be further from the crisp precision of Holbein's style, transmitted in Eworth's copy. The thick encrustations of paint, laid on during many sittings, make it seem like Auerbach is, paradoxically, burying his subjects while conveying a direct impression of their physical presence, an impression that comes directly from the paint, rather than, as with Holbein, the pose, dress and clearly rendered expression of the subject.

***Portrait of King Henry VIII*, studio of Hans Eworth, after Holbein, *c.*1560s–70s**

This silkscreen print was made by the artist Jeremy Deller in 2018. It is a version of a work first created in 1993, *Open Bedroom*, in which Deller turned his family home into an art gallery for two weeks (by appointment only) while his parents were away, replacing the objects they had bought over the years with his own art. It was a way of turning to advantage the 'slightly embarrassing' situation of living with his parents in his mid-twenties, and working from his bedroom—only years later did his parents find out.

***You treat this place like a Hotel*, by Jeremy Deller, 1993–2018**

A monumental portrait by the portrait painter Tai-Shan Schierenberg of William Burlington, son of the twelfth Duke and Duchess of Devonshire, gazes down the aptly-named Burlington Gallery, a corridor running the length of the West Wing. The gallery was created by Jeffry Wyatville for the sixth Duke, who refers to it as the 'West Gallery' in his *Handbook*, and who hung it with Old Master paintings. Schierenberg's portrait of William Burlington now looks through on to large paintings by the contemporary artists Tarka Kings and Endellion Lycett Green.

***Portrait of William Cavendish, Earl of Burlington*, by Tai-Shan Schierenberg, 1999**

North Sketch Sequence, by Jacob van der Beugel, 2014 (see page 30)

One of the boldest recent commissions at Chatsworth fills an entire corridor, known as the North Sketch Gallery, on the second floor of the house. We encounter a mysterious series of blocks, like narrow ledges, set in panels in a sequence from floor to ceiling, illuminated by light reflected from the mirrored wall opposite. They are, we quickly learn, highly coded family portraits.

The artist, Jacob van der Beugel, created these portraits by taking samples of his subjects' DNA—the building blocks of life common to all humans. The samples were translated, through the complicated process of genetic sequencing, into rows of letters, which were then used to form the shapes on the walls. The 'sequences' are the patterns of the four basic molecules that make up DNA, known simply by the letters *A*, *T*, *C*, *G*—like an alternative form of musical notation. You can't of course recognize the subjects by the pattern of blocks on the wall: the panels (from left to right, the Duke, William Burlington, Laura Burlington and the Duchess, with a central panel showing an 'Everyman'—the DNA we all share) represent them using scientific symbols and patterns. Jacob van der Beugel chose one of the oldest mediums for art—baked clay—to transform this scientific vision into something luminous with the mystery of the origins of human life and character.

To the basic DNA pattern van der Beugel added another layer, so that each portrait shows something of the sitter's personality—something particular to each of them. In the Duke's case it is his favourite walk around the garden, the meandering path of which is traced by the rough blocks on his wall. The Duchess preferred to a show a piece of music, a composition by John Rutter. Like so many of the portraits hanging on the walls at Chatsworth, the *North Sketch Sequence* shows how human character is determined not just by genetic inheritance, but also by the way we live our lives, by our experiences and by sheer luck. It is a complex idea, so unexpected in a work made of earthenware, but the effect is simple and intriguing. Instead of a puzzle to solve, the viewer finds an enigma to admire.

***North Sketch Sequence*, by Jacob van der Beugel, 2014**

The elaborate chair on the right plays Brahms's 'Wiegenlied' ('Lullaby') when somebody sits on it —perfect for the nursery, although here shown in the Private Dining Room, next to the austere form of an *Enignum Locus Chatsworth Chair*, one of twenty-four fabricated from walnut by the Irish designer Joseph Walsh in 2016, made especially for this room.

***Walnut inlaid hall chair with Swiss musical movement*, nineteenth century**

Following the commission to make initially two, then a set of dining-room chairs for Chatsworth, Joseph Walsh created this two-seater bench, using white ash and goat suede upholstery. The gentle curves of the side rests, and the soft covering, give an air of lightness and comfort, although this is a seat to remain upright on, rather than collapse into.

***Enignum Free-Form Two Seater*, by Joseph Walsh, 2015**

In a secluded part of the garden, three large cut-out figures lounge sociably around a table on which stand a bottle and two glasses. They seem nonchalant, as if having been placed in the first shady spot, but they have been positioned with the utmost care by the twelfth Duke and Duchess and Allen Jones, the artist who was commissioned to make the painted steel sculpture. Their bright red forms are visible in ever-changing configurations from different vantage points around the garden and surrounding landscape.

***Déjeuner sur l'herbe*, by Allen Jones, 2007**

In 2009 the Oak Stairs were restored to the original scheme designed by the architect Jeffry Wyatville for the sixth Duke: a grand staircase leading from the Painted Hall connecting the first Duke's house with the new North Wing. Light for the portraits that hang high on the walls is provided by a dome and lantern added in 1829, which for many years were concealed above a false ceiling. Hanging here is the Garter Banner for the eleventh Duke, originally displayed alongside other banners of living Knights of the Garter in the Quire of St George's Chapel, Windsor. According to custom, it was returned to the family following the Duke's death in 2004.

Famille rose is a term that was coined in France in the nineteenth century for a particular type of rose-coloured ceramic glaze derived from colloidal gold, or gold particles in liquid suspension.

 Plate from a Chinese Famille rose dinner service, painted with horses in a landscape, c.1736–95

The artist Michael Craig-Martin makes deceptively simple-looking images from ordinary objects, the sort of thing we encounter every day: an energy-saving lightbulb, a watch face, the lid of a plastic coffee cup; they may seem banal, but in his hands they become monumental. Craig-Martin uses colour in a striking manner, based on the straightforward observation, as he puts it, that 'anything can be any colour': the point is not naturalism but rather emotional impact, particularly when the intensity and saturation of the colour are turned right up. Colour and design come together in *Fragments* to transform the objects that surround us (but that in years to come will seem outmoded, quaint even) into romantic images of the present. This group of six screen prints is among the many works by Craig-Martin collected by the twelfth Duke and his Duchess—when asked who is their favourite contemporary artist, they are likely to say his name in unison.

***Watch, Light Bulb and Headphones, from Fragments*, by Michael Craig-Martin, 2015**

This painting, hanging in the Private Dining Room, was long thought to be a portrait of Mary, Queen of Scots by the Italian painter Federico Zuccaro. It was used by the sculptor Richard Westmacott as the model for his statue of Mary, commissioned by the sixth Duke, intended to stand on the so-called Queen Mary's Bower, ambitiously redesigned as a shrine to the Scottish Queen—until the Duke came to his senses and cancelled the scheme as 'a false sign of the romance of history'. A 1924 restoration of the painting showed that a red bead necklace and crucifix were, in fact, later additions, covering up a more worldly, glamorous pearl necklace. The subject's identity remains unknown, but it has been recently suggested that she may be Margaret of Parma (the sister of Philip II of Spain, whose portrait hangs nearby in the Private Dining Room), and have been painted by an artist in the circle of the Spanish painter Alonso Sánchez Coello.

***Portrait of a lady, possibly of Margaret of Parma*, circle of Alonso Sánchez Coello, *c.*1560**

Howard Hodgkin's four large etchings of palm trees, made using the technique of intaglio and carborundum, draw on the artist's memories of travel posters seen thirty years earlier in the Paris Métro, by artists such as Bernard Villemot and Raymond Savignac. In Hodgkin's vividly coloured prints the palm tree becomes a simple shape, like a coloured silhouette, a 'soothing, straightforward' image, as he put it, to uplift and raise the spirits.

***Palm and Window*, by Howard Hodgkin, 1990–91**

A long, uneven red band, like a kicked-about red carpet, runs along the bottom (or top, depending how you hang it) of a leaf-green field. A dark fringe marks where the colours meet and mix, above a few small splashes of red paint. John Hoyland, the Sheffield-born artist who made this painting at the beginning of his career, spent his life showing how colour and shapes could be used to create wordless dramas. The painting was owned for many years by the American collector Stanley J. Seeger, who kept it at his Surrey home, the Tudor manor house Sutton Place. It was bought by the twelfth Duke of Devonshire from one of the sales of Seeger's collection, and remains among the largest and most abstract works of modern British painting in The Devonshire Collections.

***21.2.66*, by John Hoyland, 1966**

Like a giant diamond ring attached to the wall, this mirror by the British designer Jake Phipps flings shards of light from the 750 individual sections of mirror mounted around its perimeter on to the walls of the Grotto beneath the Great Stairs.

***Stellar Mirror*, by Jake Phipps, 2010**

Eight tapestry panels by the Brussels workshop of Jacques Coenot and Jan Cobus were woven around 1690. They may well have been acquired by the first Duke of Devonshire shortly after, as Treasury Books for May 1691 attest. The travel writer Celia Fiennes saw the bright new works in the State Rooms on her visit to Chatsworth eight years later, writing in her notebook of the 'swete tapistry hangings with small figures and very much silk'. They give their name to the room in which four of the panels now hang: the Tapestry Bedroom.

47 ***Tapestry with biblical and mythological themes*, by Jacques Coenot and Jan Cobus, *c.*1690**

Among the paintings in the Tapestry Bedroom hangs a small, captivating *Head of the Christ Child* (on the door to the bathroom), brightly lit and with a mop of loose golden curls. It is a copy by an unknown artist of a detail in the *Madonna della Rosa*, by the sixteenth-century Italian painter Parmigianino, in the exaggerated, elongated style for which he was known, now hanging at the Old Master Gallery at Dresden. A red chalk drawing for the painting is kept at Chatsworth, showing Parmigianino working out the unusual composition of Christ sprawled over his mother's lap, their arms interlinked as she passes him a rose, symbolic both of purity and suffering. The striking subject and composition led to many copies and variations on Parmigianino's painting.

***Head of the Christ Child*, after Parmigianino, *c.*1530s**

Sowing Colour, a ceramic installation by Natasha Daintry, takes its place in one of the book alcoves of the Dome Room alongside the upward-thrusting figure of Mercury; brightly coloured cylindrical pots are stacked up to the ceiling, diminishing in size and proliferating in number as they ascend from shelf to shelf, according to the Fibonacci sequence of numbers, which is based on patterns of natural growth. The pots echo the variety and abundance of nature all around: we might be looking at prismatic colours reflected in the waters of the Cascade, the series of stone terraces that dominate the lawns on the east side of the house, which were designed by Monsieur Grillet, a hydraulics engineer who is said to have created fountains for Louis XIV.

Sowing Colour, **by Natasha Daintry, 2017–18**

How many umbrellas have we lost, left on a bench after the rain has stopped? And how many of these vagrant umbrellas have we found? You might miss Michael Craig-Martin's purple steel-frame umbrella, blown into the undergrowth on a blustery day. Is it a drawing in space, or a sculpture?

***Umbrella (Purple)*, by Michael Craig-Martin, 2013**

A bronze sculpture of a warthog, by the British artist Mark Coreth, is positioned in a pond at the bottom of the Ravine—a suitable habitat for warthogs, who like to be near water.

***Warthog*, by Mark Coreth, 1993**

SCENE II

TROUBLE IN ARCADIA

Rooks caw and geese honk as they fly overhead. Daffodils brighten the lawns, fresh buds adorn bare branches. It is the spring of 1957; the year is waking, and yet the house remains empty. Shutters are fastened, doors and gates are bolted. Long stone corridors, grand staircases and wooden-panelled rooms lie still and silent. A key turns in a lock and three figures enter, their conversation shaking a corner of the house into life: a man and a woman, ANDREW and DEBORAH CAVENDISH, and their guest, a thin, good-looking type with a piercing gaze and dirty fingernails, the artist LUCIAN FREUD. They pass through corridors and into large rooms, where, above the bulky forms of sheeted furniture, the visitor glimpses gilt cornices glinting in the darkness, and painted ceilings filled with scenes of Classical myth and history. Finally, they enter a room upstairs whose walls and ceiling are entirely covered with scenes of mass abduction: *The Abduction of the Sabine Women*, the Duchess says, by Thornhill, one of the last great artists to work here, in the eighteenth century. She points to the face of one of the Sabines, remarking that it looks a little like the young Queen Victoria; the artist laughs and agrees. The party continue their tour of the shuttered house.

When the young Lucian Freud stayed with Andrew and Deborah Cavendish, the eleventh Duke and Duchess of Devonshire, at their house in the nearby village of Edensor, Chatsworth had been unoccupied for over a decade. Andrew's father, Edward Cavendish, the tenth Duke, had spent much of the Second World War at Compton Place in Eastbourne, within easy reach of London where he was an under-secretary of state in Churchill's government.

The Library during the Second World War

During the war Chatsworth had been animated by the footsteps and chatter of girls from Penrhos College in North Wales, evacuated to the safety of rural Derbyshire. When they finally departed in 1946, the house was shut up once again. Nobody was sure what would happen next.

In the decade after 1945 more than four hundred country houses were demolished in Britain, and many more taken into public ownership. Grand houses were simply too expensive to run, for the most part because the agricultural land that provided their income had, since the late nineteenth century, become unprofitable. In the wake of a terrible war they also symbolized a way of life that seemed to many unjustified, and the notion that they might be kept alive by tax breaks, as was suggested in a government report of 1950, was hardly likely to gain much sympathy. Turning them into museums or destroying them were both practical solutions but also symbolic of the death of the old world order.[1]

What, then, should be done with Chatsworth? There were a number of suggestions. Francis Thompson, its librarian, suggested that the house might be transformed into an institute of art history.[2] Others thought that it might become a 'National Gallery of the North' and display items on loan from the National Gallery, British Museum and other London institutions.

The tenth Duke prevaricated, unable to take such a momentous decision. After all, the house contained some four centuries of family memories, as well as many works of art commissioned or collected by his ancestors. The problem was really about money. The house had not been renovated since the Edwardian era, and was in serious need of repairs. Evelyn, wife of Victor Cavendish, the ninth Duke (who succeeded to the title in 1908), had worked hard to conserve and clean, and in the middle of the 1930s oversaw an emergency restoration of the ceiling of the Painted Hall, which was found to be sagging by almost a foot at the centre, and on the verge of collapse.[3] Some years earlier, in 1920, the Great Conservatory—built by

The wedding of William Cavendish, Marquess of Hartington, and Kathleen Kennedy, 6 May 1944

Joseph Paxton (with architectural consultant Decimus Burton) from 1836 to 1840—had been demolished over several days using dynamite, leaving only the supporting walls. It had been neglected during the First World War, and as a result was too expensive to conserve and maintain.

The family debt did not help matters. By the time the seventh Duke succeeded to the title in 1858 the accumulated debt was just under a million pounds.[4] Investments in the industrial town of Barrow-in-Furness were made to counter this, and, for a while, seemed to help; but by the time of the seventh Duke's death, in 1891, the debt had reached £2 million, an astronomical sum for the day.[5] When the eighth Duke, Spencer Compton (the first not to be called 'William'), took over, he wrote, 'I can't say that at present I see anything to be done except to shut up Chatsworth and Hardwick.'[6] It was left to the ninth Duke to sort out the problem. Like many other landowners hit by the devaluation of agricultural estates, Victor Cavendish turned to the family's other assets.[7] Family holdings in Ireland and England were sold, as well as the Duke's London home, Devonshire House in Piccadilly (in 1919 for £750,000). Chiswick House, the pleasure villa on the outskirts of London, was sold ten years later to the local council, which used it at first as a fire station. Works from the collection were also relinquished, including exceptionally rare early printed books by William Caxton and a Shakespeare First Folio.

Victor's success in paying off debts offered some hope that Chatsworth, in the time of Edward, the tenth Duke, might survive the difficult war years, and beyond. By the late 1940s plans were afoot to open the house once again to visitors. And yet worse troubles were still to come. In November 1950 Edward, the tenth Duke, died suddenly of a heart attack while chopping wood (one of his favourite activities) at Compton Place, Eastbourne. His eldest son, Billy Hartington, had been killed by a sniper in Belgium in September 1944, while serving in the Coldstream Guards. (Only four months earlier he had married Kathleen 'Kick' Kennedy, sister of John F. Kennedy.) It therefore fell

Hardwick Hall, Derbyshire, c.1955

to the Duke's second son, Andrew, to inherit the dukedom, along with a new set of money troubles. The astronomically high estate duties of the time meant that Andrew Cavendish was obliged to hand over eighty per cent of the overall value of the family estate to the government.[8] Had the tenth Duke died just a few weeks later, according to the provisions of a trust he had established for the estate, there would have been no tax due at all. An appeal to the government failed, and there was another scramble for ideas—perhaps Chatsworth might after all become a museum.[9] Nobody was under any illusion as to what this really meant: the end of Chatsworth as a family home.

The solution, when it came, was eminently practical: to continue the sales begun by the ninth Duke but on a much greater scale. Andrew Cavendish realized that, as well as selling land in Scotland and Derbyshire, the only real option was to relinquish Hardwick Hall, widely regarded as one of the most beautiful of late-Elizabethan mansion houses still standing. With its tall glazed façades and elaborate decoration, it was also a symbol of the origins of the Cavendish dynasty in the person of its builder, the powerful and mysterious Elizabeth, known as Bess of Hardwick.[10] In the late 1940s Hardwick was still a working house, run by the Duke's grandmother, the Dowager Duchess Evelyn, widow of the ninth Duke, 'a rather careful housekeeper', as she described herself in a letter to Francis Thompson.

Prized works of art had also to be sacrificed. The four *Devonshire Hunting Tapestries*, showing otters, bears, swans, deer and boars being hunted amid spectacular foliage and scenery, which had been woven in northern France in the fifteenth century, and probably bought by Elizabeth Hardwick in the sixteenth century, were acquired by the Victoria and Albert Museum. A large drawing, or 'cartoon', of Henry VII and Henry VIII by Hans Holbein the Younger, a study for a wall painting covering an entire wall in the Privy Chamber at Whitehall Palace, which was destroyed in 1698, went to the National Portrait Gallery. *The Donne Triptych*, a fifteenth-century altarpiece

The Donne Triptych, by Hans Memling, 1470–78

by Hans Memling, showing the courtier John Donne and his wife Elizabeth Hastings kneeling in reverence of the Virgin and Child in a lush landscape setting, was secured by the National Gallery. It was joined there by *An old man in an armchair*, then thought to be by Rembrandt, now thought to be probably by Rembrandt. The British Museum benefited from a tenth-century illuminated manuscript, the *Benedictional of St Æthelwold*, made for the Bishop of Winchester, and one of the greatest painted books surviving from Anglo-Saxon England—it now resides in the British Library—as well as the *Liber Veritatis*, a book of two hundred drawings by the French artist Claude, documenting his own paintings for the purpose of preventing forgeries, and a sketchbook by the Flemish artist Anthony van Dyck, both of which had been originally acquired by the second Duke of Devonshire.

Most striking of all, the British Museum also received one of the greatest treasures at Chatsworth: a bronze head of Apollo dating from the fifth century BC. *The Chatsworth Head*, as it is known now, was found attached to its body in the bed of the River Pediaeos in central Cyprus early in the nineteenth century. The bronze statue was placed in an oxcart and dragged over the gravel of the riverbed by the locals who had discovered it, causing the limbs and the head to fall off. The finders gathered them up anyway, tossing them in sacks to complete the journey.[11] Most of the Apollo was sold as old copper scrap metal. Only the head and one of the legs were to survive: the head was bought by an English collector, who, in March 1838, sold it to the sixth Duke of Devonshire.[12] The leg found its way to the Louvre. Very few original bronze sculptures survive from Ancient Greece—what we know of them today is almost entirely through copies made in marble—making this example from the high moment of Greek art all the more significant, and its breaking-up after more than two thousand years all the more tragic.

Reproduction of
The Chatsworth Head

Hardwick was gone, and eight treasures had been carried away, but the debt problem was on its way to being solved. The dust was settling—and it seemed that Chatsworth had been saved after all.

And yet the Herculean task of renovating the house, making it fit for occupancy—as well as viable for a paying tourist trade that would allow the house to stand on its own two feet—had only just begun. In 1955 Andrew and Deborah Cavendish took the decision to move back into Chatsworth—a sign of optimism but also of almost reckless bravado, considering all that needed to be done: cleaning, painting, papering, fixing, darning, upholstering, plumbing, wiring, refurnishing and rearranging. Stores were scoured for all manner of objects: lamps, chairs, mantlepieces, wood, glass, marble, textiles, many of which had been rescued from other, former Cavendish houses.

There was also the art collection to consider. Very little had been acquired since the mid-nineteenth century. The seventh Duke had added some important books on horticulture and natural history to the Library, including Daniel Giraud Elliot's beautifully illustrated folio *A Monograph of the Paradiseidae; or, Birds of Paradise*, printed in London in 1873, and works by the Victorian naturalist John Gould, including his illustrated account of the mammals of Australia. Such large, luxurious volumes embodied the latest scientific findings, as well as aesthetic advances in commercial book production in the form of brightly coloured, hand-painted lithographs. But it was only in the 1950s, when Andrew and Deborah Cavendish moved in, that the older tradition of collecting and commissioning recent and contemporary art started up once again. Early-twentieth-century paintings by Walter Sickert and Henry Tonks were among the many modern British works bought by Andrew, alongside works by artists associated with the Bloomsbury circle, notably Duncan Grant (who was a fairly frequent guest at Chatsworth and made paintings of the interior) and Vanessa Bell. Two large watercolours by Samuel Palmer—illustrations for John Milton's poem *Il Penseroso*, among

Woman in a White Shirt,
by Lucian Freud, 1958–61

the greatest of Palmer's glowing, Arcadian images of the English countryside —were acquired in the mid-1970s, bought relatively cheaply at a time when many forgeries were surfacing.

Some of Andrew Cavendish's more contemporary purchases might have seemed challenging, at least by the standards of the time—a painting by L.S. Lowry, for example, or a drawing by Dora Carrington titled *A Man with a Bowl on His Head*. Odd, perhaps—but then dukes and duchesses themselves were increasingly seen as oddities in the new democratic age of television and space travel. 'Poor old Dukes,' Andrew wrote in his memoir, 'considered more freakish by the day.' And then there was the question of who to commission to paint up-to-date portraits of family members, to hang alongside ancestral portraits from the hands of great artists such as Reynolds and Gainsborough?

In 1954 Andrew had commissioned the Italian portrait painter Pietro Annigoni to paint Deborah, showing her in a red-lined blue cloak in a landscape setting, in the manner of Italian artists since the time of Leonardo (and Flemish artists before him). Lucian Freud was less than complimentary about Annigoni, whose attempt to paint like Leonardo, but 'in the modern way, with a Horlicks mixing machine, or something' to get the 'Leonardo look', was as unlike the style of his own portrait of Deborah, completed several years later, as could be imagined.[13]

In 1950 Freud made a small portrait on copper of Andrew's sister, Elizabeth Cavendish, one of his best early paintings. Freud had first come across Elizabeth when he designed an Arcadian costume for her—'a sort of shepherdess... a white dress with a belt and some flowers', he later recalled—his only costume design.[14] Freud's painting of Deborah, however, marked a new stage in the development of his style.

The Duchess began visiting Freud's studio along the Regent's Canal in London for morning sittings in 1958. The painting progressed slowly,

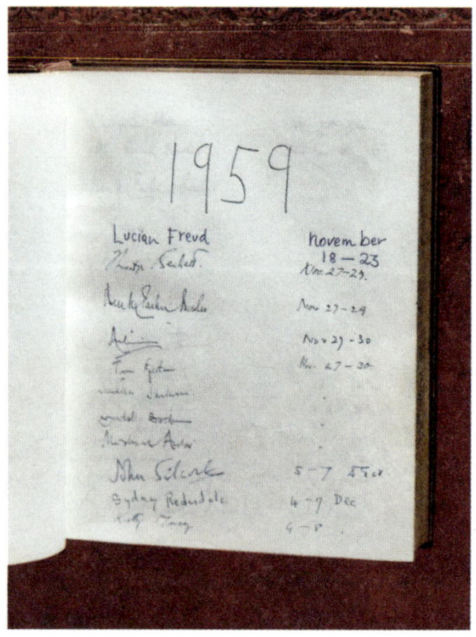

Guest book, 1959–83

but the image that emerged must have surprised even Freud himself. Gone were the refined, thin brushstrokes of the little picture of Elizabeth Cavendish; in their place were thickly wrought strokes, fleshy and textured, using all the richness and sensuousness of oil paint. This style of painting seems to lay bare the psychology of Freud's sitters, their inner life laid out on the surface of the canvas, encoded in a drama of brushstrokes. *Woman in a White Shirt*, as the painting was called, as if titles and social rank meant nothing (which was hardly true for Freud, ever keen to develop friendships with members of the British aristocracy), shows the Duchess looking thoughtful and a little troubled, perhaps pondering the problems Chatsworth faced in these years. It was, after all, at this moment that she and Andrew had decided to move back in, and they were under no illusions as to the scale of the task before them.

Work had begun in 1958 to renovate the family's apartment in the house—an 'army' of workmen had arrived and were 'making a great deal of dust and noise', Deborah wrote.[15] By November of the following year the family were finally able to move in. The first name to appear in the visitors' book was that of Lucian Freud, who stayed for six days at the end of the month. He marked the opening of the house by making a wall painting in the small bathroom next to the much larger Sabine Room, decorated with James Thornhill's murals *The Abduction of the Sabine Women*.

A famously slow worker, Freud spent his days painting three cyclamen flowers, with leaves, stems and buds, the only part of the mural he completed. When the other house guests returned from the day's pheasant shoot, they were greeted by the appearance of just a few more petals, or one additional stalk. It might not have seemed much for a day's work—certainly, to have covered the rest of the walls and ceiling, as Thornhill had next door, would have taken him months, if not years. But, for the time being, it was enough—a symbol of new beginnings, new friendships, a new era for the house.

When visiting Russia as Ambassador Extraordinary at the coronation of Nicholas I in 1826, the sixth Duke had been shown a fountain which the Tsar claimed threw the tallest jet in the world. The Tsar's pride in his fountain clearly made an impression—seventeen years later, in anticipation of a visit from Nicholas I to Chatsworth, the sixth Duke set Joseph Paxton and his clerk of works, Benjamin Holmes, to work building a new water jet at the north end of the Canal Pond to rival that of the Russian Tsar. The natural setting of the house next to a steep rise of land provided the water pressure, which, according to Paxton, drove the jet to a height of almost three hundred feet.

65 ***Emperor Fountain*, designed by Joseph Paxton, 1843–4**

Eugénie Sellers Strong, the archaeologist and art historian, and former librarian at Chatsworth, describes this fragment of a Roman relief, carved with a 'singularly fresh surface', in her celebrated 1907 book on Roman sculpture: 'On it are four soldiers in military undress, two to the right and two to the left of the officer in their midst. The foremost man, who is also the most completely preserved, carries on his left shoulder a large circular book-box—a sort of *scrinium*—into which are loosely thrown a number of tablets. The next, whose head is also preserved, though the nose is broken and the head itself has been broken off and replaced, carries with both hands a pile of similar tablets.'[16] She identifies the scene as showing Hadrian's famous remission of all taxes and debts owed to the state by individuals in AD 118.

Roman marble relief fragment **(detail), Hadrianic, *c.*AD 118–38**

Sheaf of Light, shown here in the Grotto beneath the Great Stairs, seems to bring together three disparate things: the substance of which it is made, white marble; the form it has taken, roughly that of a leaning sheaf of grain stalks; and the idea that one might symbolically gather together beams of light. The surface of the marble is animated by ridges, capturing the real, rather than symbolic, light that falls over the surface of the standing marble block—in fact, two joined blocks. It is a moment crystallized and preserved, colliding the immediacy of light with the unimaginably slow time of geological formation, and with the long, patient work of carving marble.[17]

 ***Sheaf of Light*, by Tim Harrisson, 2004**

Caius Gabriel Cibber was a Danish sculptor who had been employed by Sir Christopher Wren during his work rebuilding the City of London after the Great Fire of 1666. His most important works at Chatsworth are the two figures of *Faith* and *Justice* in the Chapel, carved in alabaster, but he also worked continuously from 1688 making statues for the numerous fountains created for the first Duke's house, including the Venus Fountain, the Willow Tree Fountain, and the Neptune and Sea Horse Fountains. Of these only the Sea Horse Fountain remains. For it, Cibber carved five rearing horses with wings and sea-serpent tails, and a figure of Triton, all from stone extracted from the quarries at Roche Abbey in Yorkshire.

***Sea Horse Fountain*, by Caius Gabriel Cibber, 1688–91**

An old man with a wizened face, wearing a white turban and a fur-lined robe fastened by a weighty gold clasp, peers out at us quizzically from the wall of the small gallery known as the Old Master Drawings Cabinet. Who is he? In the darkened background, a snake curls around a gilded column, topped with the head of a lion—could this be Moses or Aaron, both associated with the symbol of a snake in the Bible? Or could the blotchy skin of the man indicate that he has leprosy, and that this is King Uzziah of Judah, whose punishment for overstepping himself and acting as a priest in the local temple was to be afflicted with that degenerative disease? Or might we even speculate that this is Rembrandt himself, looking out at us with the searching, doubting expression often seen in his self-portraits?

***A man in oriental costume*, by Rembrandt, *c.*1639**

In the early 1900s Walter Sickert painted a number of nudes reclining on iron bedsteads, in cheap lodging rooms in Camden Town, North London. The figure in this painting lies on a violet counterpane, one arm and both legs dangling over the side in a strange, seemingly uncomfortable pose. Sickert composes his scene in broad strokes and dabs of paint, creating strong contrasts of light and dark. A patch of red in the upper right gives an air of unexplained menace. A few years later Sickert made a group of paintings of nudes in similar interiors in connection with the 'Camden Town Murder'—the killing of Emily Dimmock in September 1907. This painting was bought by Andrew Cavendish, the eleventh Duke of Devonshire, in 1988.

***Nude on a bed*, by Walter Richard Sickert, *c.*1906**

Angela Conner's bronze bust of the poet John Betjeman stands in the garden alongside other portraits of family and friends, including the playwright Tom Stoppard, Lady Emma Tennant and Andrew Cavendish, the eleventh Duke, who collected and commissioned the busts from Conner, a close friend since the early 1960s. The surfaces of Conner's portraits are deeply worked, like the thickly painted canvases of Lucian Freud, whose portrait by Conner is also kept at Chatsworth. Betjeman was a companion of the eleventh Duke's sister, Lady Elizabeth Cavendish, the subject of one of Freud's earliest and best portraits.

***Sir John Betjeman*, by Angela Conner, 1973**

Freud depicts his sitter, Lady Elizabeth Cavendish, the daughter of the tenth Duke of Devonshire and a childhood friend of Queen Elizabeth II, with a thoughtful, expectant expression, as if her attention had been caught by the strains of distant music, by voices from the next room, or as if she had suddenly remembered something. Painted in thin layers on the unusual support of copper, it shows Freud scrutinizing his subject with a minute intensity of vision.

 ***Head of a Woman*, by Lucian Freud, 1950**

Lucian Freud's portrait of Deborah Cavendish, Duchess of Devonshire—*Woman in a White Shirt*—hangs above portraits of her husband Andrew Cavendish, the eleventh Duke, his sister Lady Anne Tree, the philanthropist and prison-rights activist, and his mother Mary Cavendish, Dowager Duchess of Devonshire. Together they show how Freud changed from his early, precise yet unguardedly awkward style, in the painting of *Head of a Woman*—Lady Anne Tree—from 1950, to the two more broadly brushed portraits either side, made two decades later. 'I'm always interested in a family over a period,' Freud once remarked. 'From first to last I painted them [the Cavendishes] over twenty-five years. It didn't seem like a plan.'[18]

***Woman in a White Shirt*, by Lucian Freud, 1958–61**

This is one of several detailed studies, here made in gouache, pastel and pencil, by the Scottish artist Stephen Conroy for a portrait of Andrew Cavendish that was commissioned by his son, the current Duke. Conroy was a leading light of the figurative painting movement at the Glasgow School of Art during the 1980s. The precision of his drawings and his muted palette bring to mind the portraits of Meredith Frampton from earlier in the twentieth century. The eleventh Duke is shown in his sitting room, the Lower Library.

***Preparatory study for portrait of Andrew, eleventh Duke of Devonshire*, by Stephen Conroy, 1992–3**

The interior shown in the painting on the end wall is Lucian Freud's studio in Thorngate Road, Maida Vale, a council flat where he lived and worked. The sitters are Lucie Freud, the artist's mother, sitting pensive in an armchair, and behind her lying on a divan Jacquetta Eliot, Countess of St Germans, who was at the time Freud's model and lover. A dark hillock of blanket joins the forms of the two women, covering Jacquetta's legs, and framing Lucie's portrait, yet they might otherwise be in different paintings.

At the time, Lucie was his main subject—she was recovering from a period of depression and a suicide attempt after the death of her husband, the architect Ernst Freud, son of Sigmund Freud, three years earlier. 'I started working from my mother because of my father's death,' Freud later said. Other portraits show her close up, her son studying her features with characteristic thoroughness and detachment. As viewers of *Large Interior, W.9*, we seem to be hovering above the chair on which Freud's mother sits resignedly still for her son's gaze, whereas Jacquetta reclines on our eyeline, enjoying the act of modelling. Freud's portraits of Jacquetta, lying naked on his bed next to a painting table, clenching her fists, sum up the intensity of their relationship, a love affair while she was married, leading to a child with Freud (not unusual for him), and an attempt to cohabit, which didn't work out—'Lucian never helped out. Never,' she told his biographer.[19]

Large Interior, W.9 seems likes an allegory for the different stages of life, of love and death—Lucie looks to the past, to her life with her husband, her eyes downcast and watery. We might imagine her tapping her wedding ring on the arm of the chair as she goes over the memories. Jacquetta is looking with an open gaze, in all the frankness of her nudity, thinking perhaps of her recent child with Freud and of the overwhelming nature of love, of its troubles and joys. Freud himself was uninterested in such symbolism (a bit too close to the work of his grandfather, which he appreciated largely for the royalty cheques from Sigmund Freud's published works that funded his gambling and contributed to the maintenance of his numerous children). He talked rather about the inspiration of a painting by the Venetian artist Giorgione, *La Tempesta*, a stormy landscape on the outskirts of a town in which a mother incongruously feeds a baby sitting on a bank of grass, while a male figure holding a staff looks on. In truth there is little in *Large Interior, W.9* that brings Giorgione to mind, aside from the mysterious relationship between the two figures, and the sense in which the paint itself is the subject: in Giorgione's case the rich colours; in Freud's case the thick and broad brushstrokes that mark his late style, defining contours and tones and differentiating textures, the pallid stretch of Jacquetta's skin and the soft heaviness of Lucie's woollen outfit. Everything seems to be painted in a thoughtful, self-evident manner, avoiding any feeling of personal expression.

Freud often talked about his laborious approach to painting, as if through his application of willpower, of brute examination, he might overcome what he perceived to be his natural lack of ability. *Large Interior, W.9* is laden with this literalness, down to the pestle and mortar that rest beside the chair on which Lucie sits. It is a wilful rejection of any 'Freudian' associations, placed not to symbolize some psychological relationship with his mother, and his lover, but rather as evidence of the way he would mix crushed charcoal with his paint to capture the colour and quality of London grime.[20]

Lucian Freud was one of the first house guests at Chatsworth after Andrew and Deborah, the eleventh Duke and Duchess, moved in. The artist spent much of his stay painting cyclamen flowers, leaves and stems on the wall of the bathroom adjoining the Sabine Room. It was his favourite flower, he said, and he painted it often—he liked the dramatic way it died, suddenly giving up and collapsing. The idea, Deborah recalled, was for Freud to have painted the whole wall, but he was 'not exactly a lightning artist' (as she put it), and only a few flowers, buds and leaves were finished. Earlier that year he had painted another image of cyclamen on the wall of the dining room at Coombe Priory, in Dorset, the house he moved into with his first wife, Caroline Blackwood; there he only got as far as three leaves and a bloom.

Cyclamen wall painting **(details), by Lucian Freud, 1959**

A Monograph of the Alcedinidae, by Richard Bowdler Sharpe, 1868–71 (see page 86)

 Collection du cent espèces ou variétées du genre Camellia, by G. Fontaine, 1845 (see page 86)

Griechische Vasenmalerei, by Adolf Furtwängler and K. Reichold, 1904 (see page 86)

Flora Graeca, 10 vols. (here vol. 6), by John Sibthorp *et al.*, 1826 (see page 86)

The later years of the nineteenth century, the time of the seventh and eighth Dukes, was a quiet era for Chatsworth, although the collecting of books continued unabated. Since the time of the sixth Duke the Library had been the hidden beating heart of the house, a great repository of knowledge keeping pace with the latest scientific discoveries, particularly in horticulture and natural history. In the late 1800s this also meant the inclusion of lavish coloured plates, and many of the books collected by the seventh Duke, who had been an outstanding scholar at Cambridge, and was the founder of the Cavendish Laboratory there in 1874, showcased the wonders of nature in the latest technique of hand-coloured lithography.

Richard Bowdler Sharpe's first monograph, begun when he was twenty-one years old, on the subject of kingfishers, or *Alcedinidae*, was completed while he was librarian of the Zoological Society. It is illustrated with lithographs by the Dutch bird illustrator J. G. Keulemans, who lived and worked in England after travelling from the Netherlands to work on Sharpe's volume. The seventh Duke is also listed as a subscriber to a book by the Victorian naturalist John Gould, his illustrated account of the mammals of Australia published between 1845 and 1863, and he may well have also acquired Gould's book on toucans. Gould's earlier publications, including his five-volume *Birds of Europe*, were illustrated for the most part with hand-coloured lithographs by Elizabeth Gould, his wife, alongside a small number contributed by the illustrator and poet Edward Lear. His *Mammals of Australia* documents many animals that were soon to become extinct, including the thylacine, or Tasmanian tiger, and the white-footed rabbit rat.

The large volume *Griechische Vasenmalerei*, illustrating ancient Greek vases, is part of a series of books by the great German archaeologist Adolf Furtwängler and Karl Reichold. It was added to the collection in the time of the eighth Duke, most likely by the Chatsworth librarian Eugénie Sellers Strong, who recorded it in the catalogue of acquisitions; some years earlier she had invited Furtwängler, her former teacher in Munich, to view the collection of Greek and Roman sculpture at Chatsworth, about which he subsequently wrote a detailed scholarly article.

Many priceless volumes left the Chatsworth Library during the twentieth century, a result of inherited debts and the considerable death duties following the early death of the tenth Duke in 1950. Over one hundred books, many of them printed before 1500, went to the British Library to join their collection of incunabula (the name given to early printed books). Andrew Cavendish, the eleventh Duke, was nevertheless able to keep the tradition of book collecting alive, acquiring many valuable volumes of natural history and horticulture, including the extremely rare (only two copies are known) book on camellias, *Collection du cent espèces ou variétées du genre Camellia* (*Collection of One Hundred Species or Varieties of Camellia*), published in Brussels in 1845 and bound for Leopold, King of the Belgians, by Mlle G. Fontaine, about whom little is known. *Flora Graeca*, by John Sibthorp, in ten volumes, is one of the great works of botanic research and illustration, based on Sibthorp's journey to Greece in the 1780s to identify plants described by the Ancient Greek physician and botanist Dioskourides.

James Shirley Hibberd's *New and Rare Beautiful-Leaved Plants* is a very different kind of botanical treatise. Shirley Hibberd was a gardener and writer from East London, known for his popular books aimed at the growing number of amateur horticulturalists, particularly those who braved the soot and grime of London to create town gardens.[21] His *New and Rare Beautiful-Leaved Plants* of 1870, illustrated with striking coloured woodblock prints made by Benjamin Fawcett, was a testament to the 'recent' passion for collecting and cultivating plants for the beauty of their foliage and leaves, rather than for their flowers. Hibberd writes in the preface: 'Beautiful leaves will not elbow flowering plants aside, but will enhance their beauty by contrast, and enrich the harmony in which they play so conspicuous a part.'

***New and Rare Beautiful-Leaved Plants*, by James Shirley Hibberd, 1870**

Mammals of Australia, by John Gould, 1863 (see page 86)

 A Monograph of the Ramphastidae, or Family of Toucans, by John Gould, 1854 (see page 86)

Most likely made especially for Chatsworth, perhaps in the time of the sixth Duke, this inkstand, sitting on a desk in the Tapestry Bedroom, features a knotted pair of serpents. This is the insignia of the Dukes of Devonshire that can be found all over the house and garden—carved on the façade and on the ends of banister rails, created in stone mosaics on the ground outside, woven into tablecloths and printed at the head of notepaper.

 ***A Regency gilt-bronze-mounted Bardiglio marble inkstand*, nineteenth century**

William Nicholson was known during his lifetime as a portrait painter, although as his son, Ben Nicholson, also an artist, acknowledged, it was the ‘poetic spirit’ of his still lifes and landscapes that was his real achievement. The delicacy and sensitivity of his painterly touch looks back to the paintings of Manet, and to Velázquez before him, both painters whom Nicholson admired, and whose debt can be seen in this painting, acquired by the eleventh Duke, of white tulips in a blue glaze jug shown to great effect against a black drape with trimmings.

***White tulips*, by William Nicholson, 1912**

Originally an open colonnade, the Chapel Corridor was created by the sixth Duke as one of three galleries running around the courtyard at the centre of the house. It is now used to display antiquities, including a colossal foot with a sandal (see page 339), and two large antique busts shown here on the right: one of the Emperor Domitian from the time of his reign AD 81–96, and further back a bust of the beautiful Antinous, the young lover of the Emperor Hadrian, made around AD 130–38, during the latter part of his reign. They look quizzically down on two large mineral specimens, a pointed crystal of quartz and a dark purple amethyst geode from Brazil.

With her powerful lion's head, Sekhmet was one of the most fearsome of Ancient Egyptian goddesses. More than five hundred figures representing Sekhmet were carved from dark granite around 1400 BC and placed in the temple devoted to the Theban goddess Mut at Karnak, at the behest of the Pharaoh Amenhotep III. There they remained for over three thousand years, until, in the nineteenth century, many of them dispersed to art collections around the world, some arriving at English country houses: at Didlington Hall in Norfolk and Kingston Lacy in Dorset, or supporting a garden bench at Trewithen House in Cornwall. It was from the collection amassed by the pioneering Egyptologist William John Bankes that the sixth Duke acquired the two Sekhmets for Chatsworth, placing them in the Rose Garden—a far cry from Thebes.

99 *The goddess Sekhmet enthroned*, **eighteenth Dynasty, *c.*1390–1353 BC**

The spectacular swirls and patterns of malachite were popular in nineteenth-century Russia, after the discovery of large quantities of the green mineral at Nizhny Tagil in the Ural Mountains. This unusually large clock is inscribed on the base *A Gift from the Emperor Nicholas 1844*—the year the Russian Tsar visited England and was entertained by the sixth Duke with a grand breakfast at Chiswick House. The clock, which shows Peter I heroically coming to the aid of shipwrecked sailors, was included in nine packing cases filled with malachite objects that were sent by the Tsar to Devonshire House later that summer.

***Bronze and malachite clock with a figure group of Peter I*, Russian, *c.*1840**

After the departure of the painters Willem van de Velde and his son for England in 1672, Ludolf Bakhuizen was the leading marine painter in Holland of his day, well known for his dramatic compositions and care in depicting the changing conditions at sea. For many years this painting was hanging at the Cavendish family home of Lismore Castle in Ireland, darkened by time and unrecognized, until it was identified by Charles Noble, the Curator of Fine Arts at Chatsworth. After restoration, it was confirmed as a work by Bakhuizen by the signature and date, 'L.B. 1678', painted on a piece of driftwood in the foreground.

103 ***A ship in stormy seas*, by Ludolf Bakhuizen I, 1678**

SCENE III

AMBITION IN ARCADIA

Chatsworth is alive with excitement: it is a clear cold day in December 1843. A twenty-one gun salute and the echoing boom of heavy cannons, positioned around the Hunting Tower on the wooded slope behind the house, announce the arrival of a royal cavalcade: QUEEN VICTORIA and PRINCE ALBERT. At the entrance gate they are welcomed by the sixth Duke, WILLIAM CAVENDISH, beaming at the visitors to his house, which he has spent more than two decades reshaping and rebuilding. After dinner, Queen Victoria and Prince Albert, the DUKE OF WELLINGTON and their host progress in an open carriage through the central aisle of the Great Conservatory, the largest glasshouse in Britain, and one of the wonders of the age. It is the work of JOSEPH PAXTON, the famous head gardener at Chatsworth, who greets the royal carriage on its arrival. The great glass roof is supported by thirty-six thick cast-iron columns, holding aloft a central nave high enough for the grandest of palm trees, the *Corypha umbraculifera*, and the Brazilian *Araucaria araucana*, or monkey-puzzle tree. The Great Stove, as it is sometimes called, is illuminated by twelve thousand hanging lamps, transforming it into a realm of magic in the midst of the Derbyshire hills.

The sixth Duke, known in the family as 'Hart'—short for the Marquess of Hartington, the courtesy title of the Duke's eldest son—devoted much of his life to Chatsworth. His right-hand man, Joseph Paxton, transformed the estate and garden: in addition to building the Great Conservatory, he planted the Pinetum and Arboretum, and had enormous boulders moved to create the sprawling Rockery. ('The spirit of some Druid seems to animate Mr Paxton

The Great Conservatory,
designed by Joseph Paxton, 1836–40

in these bulky removals,' Hart wrote.) The impressively high Emperor Fountain, also Paxton's work, was built in anticipation of a visit by Tsar Nicholas I of Russia. On this occasion, the Tsar failed to turn up, but the fountain remains named in his honour.

While Paxton reshaped the surrounding garden, Hart transformed the building. It was a house he loved, and rearranging its contents was his chief source of happiness. 'O Chatsworth,' he wrote in his diary, his words like a lover's sigh. In 1818 he engaged the architect Jeffry Wyatville to design a long series of rooms to the north of the house, including the Great Dining Room, Sculpture Gallery and Orangery, the whole culminating in the lofty Belvedere —a three-storey tower topped with a Ballroom (the decorative ceiling was painted by Pugin's collaborator John Gregory Crace) and, above, a viewing terrace, which in its elevation echoed the tall architecture of Hardwick Hall. Chatsworth metamorphosed from a traditional, box-like palace into something more like a majestic, ocean-going ship.

Hart set down his impressions of his completed house in a book, written in the form of a letter to his sister Harriet, which was privately printed in 1845 as *Handbook of Chatsworth and Hardwick*, or the *Handbook* for short. He dwells in loving detail on each room, memories surfacing at every turn. In the Drawing Room on the first floor he recalls dining with the future Tsar Nicholas I; and here also the actor David Garrick was entertained, and the famous German soprano Gertrud Elisabeth Mara sang.

The Chatsworth that had been rebuilt from the Elizabethan house at the start of the eighteenth century held little interest for him. The grand State Rooms on the second floor were best only as a 'museum of old furniture and a walk in bad weather'.[1] It was rather in his new Chatsworth that the sixth Duke preferred to spend his time.

On cold and wet days in the early spring, or during the snows of winter, Hart was happiest in his new Library. He had inherited a passion, a mania even,

Illumination from Mystère de la Vengeance de Nostre Seigneur, by Eustache Marcadé, *c.*1468

for book collecting from his father, the fifth Duke, and from his mother, Georgiana Cavendish. Hart turned the Library at Chatsworth into one of the greatest country house libraries in England, exceeded only by the celebrated library at Althorp, the creation of his uncle, George Spencer, Georgiana's brother. The library of the experimental physicist Henry Cavendish arrived in the early years of the century, and it included valuable early editions of Galileo and Copernicus. 'Booking', Hart would write in his diary, meaning that he had spent the day arranging and 'settling' books on their shelves, which presumably also involved many hours poring over their contents. Learned visitors might be shown the oldest Florentine edition of Homer's *Odyssey*, or the Anglo-Saxon *Benedictional of St Æthelwold*. Hart made several important purchases when, in the summer of 1812, the famous sale of the Duke of Roxburghe's library took place. Among them were a Shakespeare First Folio; the mystery play *Mystère de la Vengeance de Nostre Seigneur*, written for Philip the Good, Duke of Burgundy, and illuminated for his successor, Charles the Bold; what became known as the 'Chatsworth Chaucer', a manuscript copy of the *Canterbury Tales* on fine parchment from the mid-fifteenth century; and a copy of William Caxton's translation *The Recuyell of the Hystoryes of Troye,* the first book printed in the English language, which was once owned by Elizabeth Woodville, Edward IV's White Queen.

His books may have been antiquarian, but the sculpture in his new gallery was a vision of the best of contemporary art: works by artists he had discovered while travelling on the Continent, as well as those he acquired or commissioned in Rome during the 1820s. Carvings by the Italian Antonio Canova, the greatest of all the Neoclassical sculptors, with their smooth, clear forms, inspired by the art of Ancient Greece and Rome, took pride of place. The Sculpture Gallery was effectively built as a shrine to Canova's work, and to that of his pupils in Rome, and as a testament to his friendship with Hart: busts of the two men rest in niches on either side of the door. A set of

A seated figure of Madame Mère,
by Antonio Canova, 1808

Canova's tools, including a new type of chisel invented by the artist, supposedly imitating tools used by Ancient Greek artists, is also preserved in a small cabinet in the Sculpture Gallery.[2]

Hart first encountered Canova's work while visiting St Petersburg in 1817, where he attended the marriage of the future Tsar Nicholas and Princess Charlotte of Prussia. He saw sculptures in the Winter Palace carved with such perfection, as he wrote in his 'Thought Book', that the marble seemed transformed into living flesh.[3] Among them was a beautiful male figure of Paris, as well as a marble of Hebe, the Greek goddess of youth. It is hardly surprising that Hart was so smitten—they are generally agreed to represent the summit of Canova's art.

On his journey back from Russia, in Munich, Hart viewed Canova's most celebrated work, a marble group showing the three Graces—Euphrosyne, Aglaea and Thalia, the daughters of Zeus—vying with each other, in a state of undress, to be the most beautiful and seductive. The *Three Graces* had been commissioned by the former Empress of France, Joséphine, but she died before setting eyes on it. By the time Hart arrived in Munich, it belonged to her son, Prince Eugène Beauharnais—it would eventually end up in St Petersburg, joining other statues by Canova in the imperial collection. Canova had just finished another version of the *Three Graces*, commissioned in 1814 by John Russell, the sixth Duke of Bedford, who housed it in a temple, designed by Jeffry Wyatville, at Woburn Abbey. All this was bound to arouse Hart's interest, if not his envy. He secured his first works by the artist in Paris, in 1818, beginning with the grand, and rather intimidating, seated portrait of Napoleon's mother, *Madame Mère*. 'First acquired treasure!' Hart wrote. (He shared with Canova—and with many others of his time—a romantic weakness for the imperial glamour of the fallen Napoleon.)

Hart first went to Canova's studio in Rome in 1819, following an introduction from his stepmother, Elizabeth Cavendish—previously

Chatsworth from the South-East,
by William Cowen, 1828

Lady Elizabeth Foster—who had ten years earlier acquired the family name after marrying the widowed fifth Duke. 'He is delightful,' Elizabeth wrote to Hart, 'and gives the idea of what the great artists were in 1500.'

On the eve of his departure for England, Hart commissioned a bold sculpture from his new friend: one that would surpass all others, the subject and scale of which he left entirely up to the artist. It was a highly original gesture: for the most part, since Antiquity, artists were considered secondary to those who employed them to realize their grand projects or glorify them personally. Hart anticipated a form of patronage and support in which freedom was given to the artist as a way of bringing out their best. He estimated that, with his hands so untied, Canova was likely to achieve something as great as the *Three Graces*, if not better.

His appetite was whetted by a letter from his stepmother, after she saw the work in progress a few months later. 'It lives, it breathes, all life, & youth, & beauty,' she effused. When he finally saw it himself in Canova's studio, in the winter of 1822, Hart entirely agreed—it was the languid, dormant form of Endymion, the shepherd cast into eternal sleep by the moon goddess Selene. 'The quality of the marble is so fine, so hard, so crystalline, that Canova would not change it on account of the stain in the arm; that on the cheek he liked, and thought it represented the sunburnt hunter's hue,' he wrote on his return to the colder climes of Derbyshire.[4]

As with so many of the works he commissioned, the *Endymion* was bound up with deeply personal feelings, in this case those of deep sadness. In October 1822 the painter Gaspare Gabrielli, Hart's agent in Rome for buying and commissioning sculpture, had written to inform the Duke of Canova's death in Venice. Canova had not considered the *Endymion* entirely finished, although any other artist, Gabrielli added, might have considered it so. 'It was with mingled feelings of grief and exultation, of boundless admiration and recent bereavement, that I first saw my group in the well-known studio,'

Reclining Bacchante, by Lorenzo Bartolini, early 1830s

Hart wrote, 'where I had passed so many happy hours with the most talented, the most simple, the most noble minded of mankind.'[5]

During this second trip to Italy, in the wake of Canova's death, Hart embarked on what has been described as an 'orgy of sculpture buying' to fill what would become his new Sculpture Gallery, work on which had begun in 1820.[6] Hart followed Canova's advice in buying or commissioning works from the sculptor's pupils and assistants—such as the copies of the crouching lions from Canova's 1792 monument to Pope Clement XIII in St Peter's, sculpted by Francesco Benaglia and Rinaldo Rinaldi, which would arrive at Chatsworth in December 1825. With Gabrielli, Hart visited the studio of just about every other Neoclassical sculptor of note in Rome at the time. From the Danish artist Bertel Thorvaldsen, Hart ordered a version of the recently completed *Venus with an Apple*—'a perfectly beautiful woman', he noted, yet 'not at all a Goddess'. Thorvaldsen's pupil Rudolf Schadow created a version of his famous *Filatrice; or Spinning Girl.* The Florentine sculptor Lorenzo Bartolini made a copy of the *Medici Vase*, a huge Ancient Greek carved vessel, kept in the Uffizi Gallery in Florence. From Bartolini, Hart also commissioned an original sculpture, a *Bacchante*, a languidly posed nymph-follower of the god of wine.

Just as alluring were the marble plinths on which the sculptures stood, when finally arranged in the Sculpture Gallery in the 1830s.[7] Hart's interest in the different impressions and effects of coloured marble verged on obsession. 'The love of marbles,' Hart wrote, recalling his visits to the ateliers of artists in Rome, 'possesses one like a new sense.' As he travelled abroad he picked up pieces of marble and had them conveyed to Chatsworth, where he would eventually find the perfect place to 'settle' them. One, in particular, was special for having been taken from the sacred site of Santa Sophia in Constantinople, and was used to decorate the floor of a window alcove in the Mineral Room, where his mother's geological collection was housed, although he later confessed to having forgotten which marble specimen it was.

Dom Pedro's Emerald, 1,384 carats

Hart made his own additions to the mineral collection, although unlike his mother he bought in bulk, and on the basis of appearance rather than scientific value. One of his major hauls was from the collection of Alexander Crichton, the personal physician of Alexander I of Russia, whose hoard numbered some four thousand specimens gathered with such purity of taste, as a report on the sale recorded, that every single rock could be described as valuable and rare. Among Hart's other purchases were obsidian from Mexico, rubellite 'of great rarity' from Ceylon, native gold from Transylvania and amethysts from Siberia. Undoubtedly his greatest acquisition, in 1831, was a deep-green crystal of emerald, considered the largest and finest uncut example in the world at that time; it came from the world-famous Muzo Mine in Colombia, and had been brought to Europe by the former Emperor Dom Pedro I of Brazil. The 'Emperor's Emerald' became the 'Duke's Emerald' and was shown to widespread amazement at the Great Exhibition in the Crystal Palace, designed by Joseph Paxton, two decades later.

The Sculpture Gallery was built to Wyatville's designs over a period of some twenty years, during which time the Duke's acquisitions began arriving at the house. They were scattered around various rooms, before finally being assembled in their new gallery in the middle of the 1830s.[8] The simple, monumental proportions of the gallery, built with milky tea-coloured local sandstone, provided the perfect setting, with the great granite *tazza*, like an oversized goblet or a fountain bowl—commissioned by Hart from the German stonemason Christian Gottlieb Cantian in Berlin—dominating, rather obstructively, the centre of the gallery. The copies of Canova's lions, asleep and awake, ordered by Hart during his 'orgy of sculpture buying' were placed on marble plinths to either side of the connecting door to the

The Orangery, early 1900s

Orangery, and under niches that housed the companion busts of the Duke (by the Scottish artist Thomas Campbell) and of Canova (by the Italian Rinaldo Rinaldi). Coloured marble columns positioned around the gallery provided dashes of brightness, relieving the monotony of white marble and sandstone. Canova's idealized portrait of the Italian poet Petrarch's beloved Laura was placed on a 'rose-red alabaster support', which itself rested upon a flecked green column of verde antico, personally excavated by the Duke's stepmother, Elizabeth, in the Roman Forum.[9]

For Hart, the Sculpture Gallery was an evocation not only of Canova and his sculpture but of Italy itself—its pure blue skies and the pursuit of pleasure.[10] 'The finest Italian day, true Chatsworth summer,' he wrote in his diary on arriving in Derbyshire on a brilliant day in 1833. The last of Canova's statues to arrive at Chatsworth was that of Hebe, lifting her ewer to pour more wine for the gods—a version of the statue that Hart first saw in St Petersburg when he travelled there in 1817. She stood at the far end of the Sculpture Gallery from the Great Dining Room, presiding over the Arcadian assemblage, and around her languorous form wafted the scent of four orange trees, orchids and other rare specimens, displayed in the Orangery beyond.

It was not by daylight that the assorted company of marble came truly alive, however, but rather in the shadowy realm of night. Two vast chandeliers illuminated the room; flickering candles rested upon porphyry and marble tables, while others still were given as torches to guests, the dancing flames mingling with the moonlight streaming through the skylights. The bodies of Canova's *Endymion*, Thorvaldsen's *Venus*, holding her winning apple, Bartolini's *Bacchante*, a bust of the famous soprano Henriette Sontag, and even the stern seated form of *Madame Mère*—'unfortunate mother of the greatest of men', as the Greek inscription on the pedestal, taken from Homer's *Iliad*, reads—all joined the visitors gathered after dinner in the early-summer evening, creating an unforgettable scene of magic and delight.

The sixth Duke ordered a version of Pietro Tenerani's tender sculpture of Cupid removing a rose thorn from his mother's foot after seeing it in the sculptor's studio in the winter of 1821. Tenerani was a pupil of Lorenzo Bartolini in Carrara, and then of the Danish sculptor Bertel Thorvaldsen in Rome, and was (as the Duke noted in his diary) 'for many years the finisher of Thorvaldsen's works'. He would in time depart from the Neoclassicism of both artists, making sculptures showing an altogether warmer, more romantic spirit, such as this rendering of the winged Cupid solicitously gazing at his mother, her hand resting gently on his chubby arm.

117 **_Cupid removing a thorn from the foot of Venus_ (detail), by Pietro Tenerani, 1823–5**

We do not know her name. Charles-Henri Cordier did not record it when he modelled and carved a portrait sculpture of this woman, around 1851, and if it has survived somewhere in a notebook or diary, it has yet to be rediscovered. When the plaster cast was turned into a bronze bust, it was exhibited under the title *Négresse des colonies* and some years later as the *Vénus africaine*.

A few years before making *Bust of an African Woman*, the twenty-one-year-old Cordier had encountered, in the studio of the sculptor François Rude, a model by the name of Seïd Enkess, a formerly enslaved man from the Sudanese region of Darfur. Enkess became Cordier's first African subject, in a bust which he titled *Saïd Abdallah, de la Tribu de Mayac, Royaume de Darfour* (*Saïd Abdallah, of the Mayac Tribe, Kingdom of Darfur*). The meeting with Seïd Enkess was a revelation for Cordier, as he noted in his diary, and the origin of his enthusiasm for sculpture as an ethnographic enterprise, recording supposedly racially determined features.[11]

Cordier's bust of Saïd Abdallah was shown in the Paris Salon of 1848, the year slavery was abolished in France for the second time. (The first abolition, in 1794, had been revoked by Napoleon in 1802.) A further bronze cast was shown in the Salon of 1850 under the title *Nègre de Tombouctou*, turning it from a portrait into a more generalized image of a black African.[12] It is not known whether he encountered the female model for his *Bust of an African Woman* in the studio of François Rude, but the following year a version of it was exhibited alongside the *Saïd Abdallah* at the Muséum d'histoire naturelle in Paris, as part of an anthropological display. That same year, both portrait busts were shown in the Austrian section of the Great Exhibition in London, and it was from here that the sixth Duke purchased them. Queen Victoria acquired two casts of the busts the following year. Some eighteen full-size versions of the *Bust of an African Woman* are known, and many smaller, decorative versions.

Cordier saw himself as part of a new world of scientific enquiry, and his sculptures as forming, as he put it, 'a new subject, a revolt against slavery and the birth of anthropology'.[13] He went on to depict other 'racial types', spending six months in Algeria, making busts of Arab, Jewish and African subjects, and later travelling to Egypt, both trips sponsored by the French state. And yet his own approach was hardly free from a belief in racial hierarchies, placing the subjects he found in Greece, for example, over those from Algeria: 'The Algerian races... do not possess the perfection of form which Greek artists found in a privileged race,' he wrote.[14] There is also little doubt that much of the appeal of his 'ethnographic' busts was decorative, and that they were admired for the clever use of materials to represent different colours of skin and fabric, as in the polychrome bust of bronze and alabaster *Man from French Sudan* of 1857. Cordier was part of the culture of Second Empire France that considered European superiority over colonial subjects as somehow natural, and which might be celebrated in 'exotic' or 'orientalizing' works of art.[15]

And yet the life-like quality of his *Bust of an African Woman* takes us beyond the politics to the sitter herself, so that we want to know more about her. How old must she have been at the time—perhaps in her late twenties? What was her position in life, having been enslaved and then freed when slavery was abolished in France? If she was a professional model, like Seïd Enkess, might we see her image in other paintings and sculptures? And what happened to her—did she live out her days in France? Did she ever see the image that Cordier had created of her? And, if so, what did she think of it?

The Italian sculptor Antonio Canova finished his marble tomb for Carlo della Torre di Rezzonico, Pope Clement XIII, in St Peter's, Rome, in 1792. The sixth Duke of Devonshire admired the tomb when he visited Rome, particularly the two lions at its base, one awake and vigilant, the other sleeping, as if they were guarding in shifts. He commissioned copies of the lions from two lesser-known sculptors, Canova's pupils Francesco Benaglia and Rinaldo Rinaldi, although he noted in his *Handbook*, in deference to his most beloved artist, that the copies give only a faint impression of the 'astonishing nature and effect of Canova's'.

***Reclining lion, awake, after Antonio Canova*, by Francesco Benaglia, 1823–5**

This green tourmaline ring, on a weighty textured mount, was designed by the celebrated London jeweller Andrew Grima for the sculptor Barbara Hepworth, an artist much admired by Amanda, the current Duchess, who bought the ring in the early 2010s.

***Tourmaline and diamond ring*, by Andrew Grima, 1970**

In Greek mythology Endymion was a shepherd who attracted the attention of Selene, the goddess of the Moon. As told by the writer Lucian of Samosata, Selene admired his beauty as he slept beneath the moon, 'with his cloak under him on the rock, with his javelins just slipping out of his left hand as he holds them, and his right hand bent upwards round his head and framing his face'. 'I'm dying of love,' she told Aphrodite, and was rewarded for her passion by Zeus, who put Endymion into an eternal sleep, so that she might visit and admire him every night. It was the perfect subject for Canova, who carved his marble Endymion, here glimpsed from behind, after being commissioned by the sixth Duke, in 1819, to create a work on a subject of his choice. It was the artist's final sculpture, brought to completion in the months before his death in 1822.

The sleeping Endymion **(detail), by Antonio Canova, 1819–22**

Reclining lion, asleep, after Antonio Canova, by Rinaldo Rinaldi, 1823–5 (see page 120)

In his *Thought Book* the sixth Duke recorded the events of his first trip to Russia in 1817, as a guest at the wedding of the Grand Duke Nicholas in St Petersburg, and then his long journey home around Europe. The pages open here record the Duke's impressions of Fontainebleau, Lyons, Nîmes and Arles, and include a recipe for 'Powder for Fumigating Rooms': 'Mix equal parts of Gum Benjamin [benzoin] and storax finely powdered—Heat a fire shovel and throw a little of the powder on it—It must smoke but not flame.' The *Thought Book* also includes an account of the Duke's second trip to Russia, in 1826, to attend the coronation of Nicholas as 'Tsar of all the Russias', and transcriptions of letters from the sixth Duke describing Nicholas I's visit to the Duke's house at Chiswick.

***The sixth Duke's Thought Book*, by William Cavendish, sixth Duke of Devonshire, 1826–45**

This small case, which is labelled *Strumenti da modellare de' quali di serviva Canova Roma 31 Decembre 1822*, contains sculpting tools used by Antonio Canova. They include a quill, a chisel for working marble, and three tools for working the clay *modelli* that were used to make the finished carvings. A collection of his tools is also preserved at the Casa di Canova at Possagno, including a drill and drill-heads, chisels, rasps and modelling scalpels. At Chatsworth they are treated like holy relics—unsurprisingly, considering Canova's status as the most famous European artist of his day. The sixth Duke acquired them on his visit to Rome at the end of 1822, following the death of Canova in October of that year.

127 ***Canova's modelling tools*, 1822**

Hand-held candles and moonlight were the preferred means of viewing marble sculptures in the evening, as guests progressed from the Great Dining Room, through the sixth Duke's Sculpture Gallery, on their way to the Ballroom in the Belvedere Tower for after-dinner entertainment. The Sculpture Gallery was the stage for the contemporary sculpture the sixth Duke had bought and commissioned from the workshops of Roman sculptors, above all that of Canova—the gallery is in essence a shrine to Canova and the influence of his beautiful, pristine marble forms. Canova's sleeping Endymion, guarded by his dog, reclines alongside a sculpture of the wounded Achilles by Filippo Albacini, at the entrance to the gallery from the dining room. In 2009 the Sculpture Gallery was returned to its original appearance at the end of the sixth Duke's life.

Lorenzo Bartolini was one of the most independent spirits of nineteenth-century sculpture, and a revolutionary by nature. The son of a blacksmith, he was raised in Florence and trained in Italy before travelling to Paris, where he studied with the great painter Jacques-Louis David. Later he became a devotee of Napoleon, making a number of portrait busts of him, and visiting him in exile on Elba. The *Reclining Bacchante* was carved on his return to Florence, at a time when he was relying on foreign commissions. The insouciant pose of the Bacchante shows Bartolini's unconventional approach to modelling—he was known for placing models in spontaneous poses, shocking his colleagues at the Florence Academy of Art. The sixth Duke thought her a 'lovely and successful production of art', even if Bartolini was to take ten years to deliver the sculpture.

***Reclining Bacchante*, by Lorenzo Bartolini, early 1830s**

The Danish artist Bertel Thorvaldsen was one of the leading sculptors in Rome in the time of Antonio Canova, carving smooth marble sculptures in the prevailing Neoclassical style. He took as his model for Venus not a living person but rather a work of art from Antiquity, the famous *Venus Victrix*, also called *Venus Holding an Apple*—she had been awarded the fruit by Paris for coming first in a beauty contest. It has been known since the late 1600s, when it was recognized as a sculpture from Roman times and restored. Shortly before Thorvaldsen carved his sculpture, the original was subjected to a controversial restoration in which the hands covered the body in an attitude of modesty; Thorvaldsen rejected this prudish nineteenth-century alteration and preserved the pose of Venus openly holding the apple in victory.[16]

***Venus Victrix*, by Bertel Thorvaldsen, 1819–21**

On 17 June 1854 the German soprano Henriette Sontag died in Mexico City, a victim of the cholera that she had contracted after singing, to great acclaim, the title role in Donizetti's *Lucia di Lammermoor* in the city's opera house. She was forty-eight years old, and touring the Americas, having emerged from retirement with the intention of restoring the fortune of her husband, the diplomat Count Carlo di Rossi, which had been swept away by the revolutions of 1848.

Even were she not a 'beautiful and fascinating woman and the greatest German singer of the century', a biographer wrote, 'the vicissitudes of her life would have furnished rich material for a romance'.[17] Sontag's 'silvery and delicious' singing voice earned her the soubriquet of 'Nightingale of the North'. She took Paris by storm in 1826, and was crowned on the stage by her admirers. Her London debut, as Rosina in *The Barber of Seville* in April 1828, caused a sensation, and was widely reported in the press: 'The audience waited in breathless suspense for the rise of the curtain; and when the fair cantatrice appeared, the excited throng could scarcely realize that the simple English-looking girl before them was the celebrated Sontag.' This was not her first singing engagement in London. One week earlier she had been invited to perform at Devonshire House. 'Such was her reputation,' one observer wrote, 'not only for musical genius, but for beauty, elegance, and fascination of every kind, that the crowds of eager spectators in the streets equalled the throng of nobility, rank, and fashion under the roof of the great *dilettante* and patron of the art, the Duke of Devonshire.'[18]

The sixth Duke was not the most likely of music-lovers. He suffered from deafness, compounded with a tinnitus that sounded, he said, like a loud coffee grinder permanently active in his ear. Yet his invitation to Henriette Sontag, who attended a number of his parties and at least on one occasion dined alone with him, was by no means uncharacteristic, or a mere passing fancy. He was an indefatigable collector, patron and promoter of the arts—sculpture, architecture, painting, music and literature alike. He attended Sontag's London debut, and noted in his diary of 1828, with characteristic brevity, 'complete success'.

Sontag was to remain in The Devonshire Collections in the form of a marble bust, made two years before she first performed in London. It was carved by Ludwig Wichmann, one of the greatest portraitists in sculpture of his time. His image of Sontag was universally admired; the German writer Goethe praised Wichmann's ability to capture the singer's individuality and character. In the autumn of 1850 Sontag visited Chatsworth and was pleased to find herself, the sixth Duke noted in addenda to his *Handbook*, displayed on the chimneypiece in the Billiard Room, alongside a bust, by Jean-Pierre Dantan, of the Italian composer Vincenzo Bellini.

The spiralling forms of these silver pails emerge from waves, resting on the entwined bodies of four dolphins, an elaborate set-up sure to enhance the experience of any bottle cooled within—when not being used as a flower vase. They were supplied to the sixth Duke in 1819–20 by Robert Garrard & Brothers, a leading London firm of goldsmiths and jewellers.

***A pair of fluted wine coolers*, by Robert Garrard, 1819**

These figures cast in lead, a copy of a famous statue group by the Flemish artist Giambologna, at one time belonged to Richard, third Earl of Burlington, and are depicted standing in his garden at Chiswick in a painting of the estate by Pieter Rysbrack.

***Samson slaying the Philistine*, probably by Richard Osgood, late seventeenth century**

This detailed ink-and-watercolour drawing shows the North Wing Wyatville designed for the sixth Duke at Chatsworth, extending out from the existing house, shown on the right, with a proposed iron railing never put in place.

 ***Designs for the West Front at Chatsworth*, by Jeffry Wyatville, 1824–5**

Originally a long gallery housing sculpture and painting, the Library as it appears now was largely the creation of the sixth Duke, who took out all the original features, with the exception of the gilded plaster ceiling and painted oval inserts, and fitted it with shelves and the appurtenances of a country house library. Here can be found the scientific tracts collected by Henry Cavendish, great albums of prints and drawings put in new bindings by the sixth Duke, large illustrated books of botany, travel literature and natural history, numerous books on art and architecture, historical works including pamphlets and tracts, a large collection of literature, poetry and drama, many editions of Classical authors in Latin, all constituting one of the largest private libraries in Britain, with more than thirty thousand books—a great gathering of knowledge standing at the heart of a house where new ideas have always found fertile ground.

Two massive vases with scalloped necks and lotus leaves carved on their bodies were a present from the Russian Emperor, Tsar Nicholas I, as the sixth Duke recorded in his diary at the end of 1826: 'My jasper things came here from the Emperor, they are very handsome, & two vases very remarkable,' he wrote. They were most likely made in the imperial factories established in the Urals, near the considerable mineral deposits discovered there in the late eighteenth century.

***One of a pair of Siberian jasper vases,* 1820**

This thirty-foot-long damask cloth for the Great Dining Room table is one of a pair at Chatsworth too large even for the industrial-size washing machines in the house, and so must be sent away to be cleaned. They are ironed when laid out on the table, a process that takes hours to ensure a wrinkle-free surface. The table setting with silver surtouts is done by members of the Conservation team, walking around the tabletop in clean socks—the final task is to iron out any footprints. Spilling red wine at dinner is one of the more serious crimes that can be committed at Chatsworth.

141 ***Damask table linen woven with the ducal crest*, nineteenth century**

The Great Dining Room, part of the sixth Duke's North Wing, is one of those high Victorian interiors on which it seems the sun will never quite set, nor the candelabras dim. Princess Victoria had her first grown-up dinner party here, at the age of thirteen, and returned as queen eleven years later. Even the figures of Bacchus leaning against the chimneypiece, two by the sculptor Richard Westmacott, are Victorian in their prudish approach to wine-fuelled abandon. The table setting, itself a work of art, is flanked by candelabra made (in the previous century) by the celebrated silversmith Paul Storr; in the middle are two great pilgrim bottles, with the maker's mark of Anthony Nelme, a silversmith from Hertfordshire active in the years around 1700. Derived from the ancient form of stoppered flasks with carrying chains, these bottles are purely ornamental, appearing as if playing the leading roles in a tabletop drama.

A bunch of *Musa acuminata*, or 'Dwarf Cavendish', bananas, has been placed on a gilded console table in the Painted Hall, in front of a large still-life painting of flowers by a follower of the French artist Jean-Baptiste Monnoyer. Two specimens of the banana plant arrived in England from China, via Mauritius, one of which was purchased by Young's Nursery for the sixth Duke of Devonshire in 1830. It was successfully cultivated by Joseph Paxton and exhibited to great success as *Musa cavendishii* at the Horticultural Society in May 1836. During the twentieth century *Musa cavendishii* and its cultivars, including Dwarf Cavendish bananas, were commercially produced, accounting for almost half of the bananas produced worldwide by the end of the century.

Georg Dionysius Ehret was born in Heidelberg in 1708, and began his life as a gardener, drawing plants in his spare time. It was thanks to his patron, the physician and botanist Christoph Jacob Trew, that he was able to devote himself entirely to botanical illustration, using gouache on paper and vellum. He would become known as the greatest illustrator of plants of his time. *Plantae selectae*, published in ten volumes from 1750 to 1773, was the culmination of the collaboration between artist and patron, and was considered one of the most important works of scientific illustration of the eighteenth century. In its final volume it incorporated the new system of plant classification devised by Linnaeus, whom Ehret had met in Holland.[19]

***Plantae selectae*, by Georg Dionysius Ehret and Christoph Jacob Trew, 1771**

For many years it was believed that this was the original greenhouse built by the first Duke in the 1690s, when the fashion for such buildings was introduced from Holland. It is now known that it was built by the third Duke in 1748, and that the first Duke's brick greenhouse, situated at the north end of the Broad Walk, was destroyed. Some of the carved stone brackets and busts ranged along the parapet belong to a group of twenty-two heads made by Henri Nadauld for the first Duke, originally placed in the courtyard at the centre of the house.

William Henry Fox Talbot, by his own account, had the idea for creating photographs while on his honeymoon on Lake Como in 1833. Returning to his house, Lacock Abbey, in Wiltshire, Talbot swiftly devised a process of fixing an image on paper using silver nitrate and salt, and a camera obscura—his 'Photogenic Drawing Process', as he called it, when he presented it to the Royal Institution in London in 1839. In competition with the Frenchman Louis Daguerre, Talbot evolved a method of shorter exposures, and the use of photographic negatives he called 'calotypes', after the Greek for 'beautiful'—*kalos*.

He soon began creating 'Photogenic Drawings' of a broad range of subjects: landscapes in France and England, still lifes, sculptures in museums and copies of works of art. These he printed in his book *The Pencil of Nature*, which appeared in six instalments from 1844 to 1846. It was published by Nicolaas Henneman, Talbot's former valet, turned photography enthusiast, who had established the first commercial photographic studio, in Reading. For many, such a publication was the first occasion of their seeing a photograph—'They are the sun-pictures themselves, and not, as some persons have imagined, engravings in imitation,' Talbot keenly pointed out in the introduction to his book. These early prints faded quickly, making this album of thirty-one photographs, assembled for the sixth Duke of Devonshire, including many plates from *The Pencil of Nature*, of such importance for its state of preservation. The photograph here shows what appears to be a cycad seed head. The album was sent to the Duke by Talbot's mother, Lady Elizabeth Fielding, after learning that he had subscribed to her son's other publication at the time, *Sun Pictures in Scotland*.

***An album of photographs*, by William Henry Fox Talbot, *c.*1845**

Only four gems by the celebrated Greek gem-engraver Gnaios survive from Antiquity. This image, carved in banded agate, complete with its original gold-ring setting, shows the Greek warrior Diomedes stealing the image of Athena from Troy—the same subject that is shown on another famous carved ancient gem, by Gnaios's contemporary Dioskourides, which was later incorporated into the Devonshire Parure.

***Diomedes stealing the Palladion*, signed 'Gnaios', *c.*40–20 BC**

In the 1830s, as he was building his large Sculpture Gallery in the North Wing, the sixth Duke also created one of the most curious new rooms in the house: a small *antiquarium*, a chamber in the West Entrance in which the sculptor Richard Westmacott and his son arranged the Duke's collection of sculptural fragments from Antiquity. The Duke had bought many from the studio of Canova after the sculptor's death; others were mementoes of his travels, or had been given to him by family and friends. Set into the section of wall shown here are small fragments of antique reliefs including, clockwise from top left, three theatrical masks set above a garland; part of a Greek votive relief to the goddess Kybele; two nymphs bathing, one looking up at the face of a satyr; and a fragment showing the three-headed Cerberus and the entwined bodies of three women. At the centre is a rare representation of the Roman goddess Juno Sospita (or 'saviour'), a patron deity of marriage and childbirth, identifiable by the goat's head skin she wears.

***West Lodge Museum: Fragment of relief head of Juno Sospita*, Roman, first century AD**

A finely-carved Roman right arm, which possibly once held a sword, is affixed to the wall like a torch-holder. Alongside is a small fragmentary head of a bearded figure—perhaps Hercules—the relatively colossal right arm becoming a symbol of his labours.

***West Lodge Museum: Right arm*, Roman, *c.*first century AD**

my heart for all your kindness and hospitality, and assure you that among your "Troops of friends", there cannot be one more obliged to you and attached to you dear James. I feel as if there were a sort of boastfulness in writing as much, even for your eye, but I cannot help it.

My dear Duke of Devonshire

Ever Faithfully Yours

Charles Dickens

The Duke of Devonshire.

Broadstairs, Kent.

Tenth October

My dear Duke of Devons

As I travelle

in the Railway carr

In 1851 Charles Dickens visited Chatsworth, a guest of the sixth Duke. Returning home on the railway, Dickens read the Duke's recently published *Handbook of Chatsworth*, a copy of which the Duke had lent him. 'It was so like going over the house again with you, and hearing you talk about it, that it had the perfect charm for me,' Dickens wrote. 'I could mention some things in it which it would require a very nice art to do as well in fiction. The little suggestive indications of some of the old servants, and old rooms—and the childish associations—are perfect little pieces of truth. I know that lingering old smell of the spirit lamp, for instance, so well!'

***Letter from Charles Dickens to the sixth Duke of Devonshire*, 10 October 1851**

The Rotherham-born William Cowen was a landscape painter in oil and watercolour, who had travelled in Switzerland and Italy early in his career. This view, commissioned by the sixth Duke, is a reminder of how steep and high is the ridge behind the house, allowing a bird's-eye view down on to the estate. The ever-practical Duke improved the ascent by the installation of stone steps.

***A view of Chatsworth from the foot of the Hunting Tower*, by William Cowen, 1828**

They have been called the grandest private stables ever built in Britain, and are rivalled only by those constructed at the same time by William Chambers at Goodwood House in Sussex, and some twenty years later by John Carr at Wentworth Woodhouse in Yorkshire.[20] James Paine's Stable Block was built for the fourth Duke, part of a great scheme of landscaping and construction around the house, which included Paine's Three Arch Bridge crossing the Derwent. The heavy rustication—the large, textured blocks of stone that make up its lower level—was an appropriate style for a building devoted to the housing of up to eighty horses, with accommodation on the first floor for coachmen, outriders, strappers (who took care of racehorses), grooms and stable boys. Surprisingly, it is larger in plan than the first Duke's house. Two carved stone stags flanking a coat of arms in the pediment above the main entrance are adorned with real antlers.

***Stable Block*, designed by James Paine, 1758–64**

On his death the sculptor Antonio Canova was rather gruesomely dismembered, his hand cut off and preserved at the Accademia di Belle Arti in Venice, and his heart placed in his monument in the church of the Frari. This white marble carving is believed to be modelled on Canova's right hand, and was commissioned by the sixth Duke from an artist whose name has not survived, a demonstration of the Duke's continued devotion to the artist whose works he valued above all others. Had Canova not died in 1822 the Sculpture Gallery might well have become a compendious museum of the Italian sculptor's work.

***Canova's hand*, artist unknown, early nineteenth century**

SCENE IV

EXILE FROM ARCADIA

t Lausanne, on the shores of Lake Geneva, GEORGIANA CAVENDISH, the Duchess of Devonshire, and her companions, including her sister HARRIET and close friend LADY ELIZABETH FOSTER, are spending the summer months. It is 1792. They are not here out of choice—Georgiana has been forced into exile by her husband, William Cavendish, the fifth Duke, for carrying the child of her lover, the Whig politician (and future prime minister) Charles Grey. The baby had been born in February, in France, given the name Eliza Courtney and bundled straight back over the water, with a wet nurse, to live with Grey's parents in England. Georgiana must remain, however, awaiting a conciliatory word from her husband. She and her companions sit in the garden of their retreat, Le Petit Ouchy, looking out over the calm lake and watching the silvery reflections of clouds drifting across the blue surface. They talk of recent events in France; word has just reached them of the storming of the Tuileries Palace, and the imprisonment of King Louis XVI and Queen Marie-Antoinette. The news is ominous: increasing unrest and rioting in Paris, massacres and atrocities—a far cry from their peaceful surroundings, where the sun warms the fresh mountain air and the mood feels light. Perhaps, with the revolutionary forces drawing closer to Switzerland, they should move further south still, over the Alps, to winter in Italy. Georgiana looks out across the lake and remembers her children, Georgiana, Harriet and William—Little G, Harryo and Hart, as she knows them. A cloud passes from the sun and warmth envelops her body. She thinks of the journey over the mountains, and the waiting reward of the blue skies and olive groves of Italy.

A Gaming Table at Devonshire House,
by Thomas Rowlandson, 1791

Georgiana married William Cavendish, the fifth Duke of Devonshire, on her seventeenth birthday, in 1774. They were ill-suited—he was reserved and taciturn, she vivacious and companionable—and their relationship soon deteriorated, even as she emerged as a leading figure in London society, the epicentre of the Devonshire House set famously satirized by the playwright Richard Brinsley Sheridan in *The School for Scandal*. The extravagant hair towers and ostrich-feathered headdresses that she popularized in the years after her marriage were a gift to the caricaturists. It was said that she was not conventionally beautiful, with heavy features sometimes described as plain, and she lamented that not even the best portrait painters captured her looks. Yet, as Horace Walpole wrote: 'her youth, figure, flowing good nature, sense and lively modesty, and modest familiarity, make her a phenomenon.'

Georgiana's renown, however, went far beyond that of a society figure. She was a political activist who canvassed for Charles James Fox, the Whig politician, in the Westminster election of 1784—even though aristocratic society poured scorn on her for pressing voters so brazenly. She was a talented writer of poetry and prose, and her anonymously published autobiographical novel, *The Sylph*, the story of an unhappy marriage, was a considerable success. Her diaries and letters are vivid historical sources, including the account she wrote of the regency crisis of 1788/9, when the 'madness' of George III raised the contentious possibility of the Prince of Wales becoming Prince Regent.

Georgiana's later life was marred by alcohol and indebtedness, as well as by the toll of her complex emotional relationships. Her close friend Lady Elizabeth Foster was the Duke's lover (and possibly also Georgiana's), and lived with them until Georgiana's death in 1806. But wherever Georgiana went, whatever she did, she was at the centre of life, by virtue of her sheer charm, energy and talent.

Head of a deer, Roman, first century AD

Despite the forced separation from her children, Georgiana's two years of exile were not entirely unhappy. Away from the suffocating protocols of the English aristocracy, she was free to pursue her interests, including mineralogy, the study of rocks and minerals that was taking on a new scientific status at the time. She collected specimens, scouring the beach at Monaco following the birth of Eliza, and conversed with scientists such as the Swiss botanist and geologist Horace Benedict de Saussure, whom she met in Geneva.[1] Georgiana wrote of her admiration for Saussure's ascent of Mont Blanc: 'he saw underneath him all the snowy points of the Mountain and rivers of Ice shining like diamonds… and the sky appear'd to him a deep prussian blue.'[2]

In Lausanne she met Charles Blagden, a leading light in experimental physics and natural philosophy. Throughout the previous decade Blagden had been an assistant to Georgiana's close friend Henry Cavendish, the reclusive pioneering scientist and grandson of the second Duke of Devonshire. Blagden organized lectures in mineralogy, from a local professor of natural history, Henri Stuve, for Georgiana and her companions. Her sister Harriet was enthusiastic, but Elizabeth Foster made no pretence about her boredom.

During Georgiana's time in exile, she gathered the minerals that were to be her most original contribution to The Devonshire Collections. As the French revolutionary forces came ever nearer, she was obliged to cross the Alps and travel down into Italy, first to Florence, then spending the winter in Rome, and finally settling at Naples, filling hotel rooms along the way with mineral samples. By the time of her arrival in the south she had acquired a substantial travelling museum. In Naples, Georgiana and her companions continued to live in style, dining at the Royal Palace of Caserta, where the Bourbon King of Naples, Ferdinand IV, presented her with a carved marble stag's head that had been found at Herculaneum. The deer's shocked expression seems to be a reaction to the destruction of the Roman town by an eruption of Vesuvius in AD 79.

The Passage of the Mountain of Saint Gothard,
by Georgiana, Duchess of Devonshire, *c.*1816

Georgiana had herself scrambled up the side of Vesuvius, hammer in hand, on the hunt for specimens. 'I have made great additions here to my collection of minerals,' she wrote to Little G from Naples. 'I shall have a most complete collection to study.'[3] While there she met the British ambassador to the Kingdom of Naples, Sir William Hamilton, an expert in volcanology also known for his collection of Greek and Roman antiquities, who had observed two eruptions of Vesuvius in the 1760s and sent samples of lava back to the Royal Society in London.

When, in August 1793, the Duke finally sent word that Georgiana would be allowed to come home, she returned with Elizabeth Foster by way of the precipitous Saint Gothard Pass in the Swiss Alps—she was later presented with a specimen of rock from the pass's highest summit by the celebrated scientist Benjamin Thompson.[4] She wrote a verse account of this dangerous crossing, *The Passage of the Mountain of Saint Gothard*, and her love of minerals proved a rich source of poetic inspiration:

> Yet 'midst those ridges, 'midst that drifting snow,
> Can nature deign her wonders to display;
> Here Adularia shines with vivid glow,
> And gems of crystal sparkle to the day.

Adularia, Georgiana explains in extensive notes appended to the poem (themselves a form of travel diary), is a fetching example of 'Feldt spar', or feldspar, a common crystallized mineral, called after the ancient name for the eastern part of the Lepontine Alps, *Adula*.

The Passage of the Mountain of Saint Gothard was first published some years later, in the Whig-supporting newspapers of December 1799. The poet Samuel Taylor Coleridge swiftly wrote a poem in response to one of its stanzas; he counters the usual, scandalous portrayals of the Duchess with

A tablet composed of Derbyshire fossils in perspective cubes, by White Watson, 1788

an ode of praise, moderated by his surprise, as well as some clear envy, that a duchess, from her position of privilege, might write such moving poetry, or describe with such feeling the story of William Tell. Georgiana's combination of a poetic response to the wilderness of the Alps with a scientific knowledge of geology and mineral formation was indeed unexpected and original. She was among the first of a new generation of Romantics to view such rugged scenery as a source of beauty; in 1802 J. M. W. Turner would sketch and paint his own impressions of the Saint Gothard Pass.

The 'peaceful science' of mineralogy provided a sort of refuge for the Duchess on her return to England, where she lived in partial reconciliation with the Duke but outside society at large. The unchanging, mute nature of rocks, with their strange, otherworldly beauty, was a source both of solace and escape. In 1798 she commissioned the Derbyshire geologist, stonemason and sculptor White Watson to remodel a grotto in the garden at Chatsworth into a crystal cave studded with fossils (the current grotto dates from the 1830s, so we can only imagine how Watson's grotto appeared). In the following year, she engaged him to continue her education, and to attempt to enthuse her children in matters of geology. He wrote a short book describing the general characteristics of minerals, their shapes and colours, as well as their feel—rough like pumice, smooth like flint or soapy like steatite, for example.[5] Stones and minerals were a Watson family obsession. White's uncle, Henry, had pioneered water-powered machinery for working stone and established the marble works at Ashford-in-the-Water, near Bakewell. His grandfather, Samuel, had been 'statuary' at Chatsworth, as White put it, making most of the highly accomplished wood and stone carvings inside and outside the house when it was built in the years around 1700.[6]

William Cavendish, fifth Duke of Devonshire,
by Pompeo Batoni, 1768

White Watson catalogued some two thousand specimens in Georgiana's collection of minerals, held both at Chiswick House and at Chatsworth. His lists include fluorite and sphalerite crystals from Ashover, toadstone from Bakewell, 'elastic bitumen' from Castleton and common coal from Chesterfield, all in Derbyshire; chalcopyrite and malachite from Ecton Hill in Staffordshire; witherite from Anglezarke in Lancashire; beautifully coloured and patterned agate pebbles from Montrose in Scotland; Alpine rock crystal and smoky quartz, as well as kyanite from Pizzo Forno in Switzerland; volcanic rocks bought by Georgiana from the collection of Dr Robert Townson (who had dedicated his 1789 work *The Philosophy of Mineralogy* to her); and vesuvianite from the eponymous volcano. One of the smallest specimens was labelled 'A stone which fell from the clouds'; at the time it was believed to have come from Mount Vesuvius, hundreds of miles away. The truth was, in fact, even more extraordinary: the pebble is a fragment of a meteorite that fell at San Giovanni d'Asso, near Siena and, as one of the first of such rocks to be identified, it helped scientists to reach the conclusion that meteorites could indeed fall to Earth from space.[7]

Georgiana's fascination with minerals, along with her talents as a writer, have often been overlooked in accounts of her life, which have seen her through the lens of her tragic relationship with the Duke, and the considerable debts that she accrued (not a patch, however, on her husband's). Meanwhile, the fifth Duke has often been characterized as a brute for his treatment of Georgiana, and for his affair with the unscrupulous Elizabeth Foster. Yet he was himself deeply interested in literature and known as a Classical scholar, who had works of Greek and Latin authors printed on large-sized paper so that he might add his own notes.[8] Books and literature formed a bond between the fifth Duke and Georgiana, as well as Elizabeth Foster: he read them sections of *Hamlet*, *A Midsummer Night's Dream* and *The Tempest*, and reportedly made them 'Shakespeare-mad'.

Bagnio and Grand Allées,
by Pieter Rysbrack, *c*.1729–30

Georgiana's collection of minerals can be seen in Chatsworth to this day, arranged in handsome, bow-fronted cabinets (designed by White Watson), with narrow, cloth-covered sloping shelves. They show her, as always, at the centre of things: along with other amateur mineral collectors at the end of the eighteenth century, she was in the vanguard of one of the greatest revolutions in the understanding of our planet and its natural history.

With the exception of the early months of her marriage, Chatsworth was never a place of great happiness for Georgiana, tainted as it was by her tempestuous relationship with her husband and his liaison with Elizabeth Foster. Georgiana had been happiest in London, where she stood at the apex of social and political life, and later at Chiswick. Here she found true escape in the grounds, with their 'velvety' lawns, statues, long alleys and hidden grottoes, as depicted by Pieter Rysbrack some decades earlier.[9] The gardens at Chiswick were as elegant and dreamlike, wrote one of her descendants, as a painting by Watteau, whose scenes of aristocratic pleasure, music-making and gallantry in ideal landscapes were the very image of Arcadia.

Thomas Gainsborough's portrait of Georgiana, made around 1785, when she was in her late twenties and at the peak of both her fame and notoriety, might well have been set in the gardens of one of her houses—most likely the long gardens behind Devonshire House on Piccadilly, a stone's throw from Gainsborough's studio on Pall Mall. Gainsborough shows the young Georgiana in a white dress with a blue sash wrapped round her waist. On her head is an enormous, broad-brimmed black velvet hat topped with ostrich feathers, a style originally designed for Queen Marie-Antoinette but one that Georgiana was to popularize in London. She holds a single pink-red rose in her wispily painted hands, and the plumpness around her chin suggests her

Georgiana, Duchess of Devonshire,
by Thomas Gainsborough, 1785–7

youthfulness at this time. Her face is fresh but rather expressionless (and may well have been finished by Gainsborough's assistant), and yet she is undoubtedly attractive, with rosy lips and soft brown eyes. Whether it is a good likeness is less certain. Gainsborough is said to have exclaimed on finishing the portrait: 'Her Grace is too hard for me!'[10]

Nobody knows how this portrait came to reside in the cottage of a Derbyshire schoolmistress, Anne Maginnis, some fifty years after it was painted. Perhaps Georgiana had given it away, unwilling in later life to be reminded of her vanished youthful beauty. But, after passing through the hands of various picture dealers, including William Agnew (who bought it in 1876 for ten thousand guineas), as well as the notorious conman Adam Worth (who stole it), and the mighty financier J. P. Morgan (who purchased the recovered work for an astronomical sum), it eventually came to Chatsworth in 1994, when it was acquired at the suggestion of the eleventh Duke. Nowadays, the portrait hangs just a few paces away from White Watson's cabinets containing Georgiana's mineral collection, in the South Sketch Gallery, built by her son, Hart, the sixth Duke of Devonshire.

Georgiana never forgot her happy days in Switzerland and Italy, which had combined a yearning for her children with her loving, but complicated, friendship with Elizabeth Foster; and, like her son after her, she treasured these memories of the freedom of travel and discovery. It was how Hart, her son, remembered her at Chatsworth: in her sanctum, known as the Den, where her writing table displayed what Sheridan described as 'organized disorder', watched over by a statue of the French philosopher Jean-Jacques Rousseau.[11] Here we might leave Georgiana, at work on the proofs of her poem, or admiring the crystal forms of a mineral by candlelight.

The Venetian painter Carriera began her career making miniature portraits designed to adorn the inside of snuff boxes. She was known in later life for her vividly engaging portraits in pastels, although she also painted miniatures of mythological scenes, often focusing on female subjects. This watercolour on ivory miniature, long thought to represent Venus and Cupid, actually shows Armida and Rinaldo, from the poem *Gerusalemme liberata* by Torquato Tasso, set at the time of the First Crusade. The beautiful Saracen sorceress Armida had been sent to kill the Christian knight Rinaldo, but instead falls in love with him. The mirror she holds alludes to the moment in Tasso's poem when Rinaldo sees his reflection in a shield and escapes from Armida's spell.

***Rinaldo and Armida*, by Rosalba Carriera, *c.*1720**

White Watson, the mineral expert appointed by Georgiana to catalogue and arrange her collection, commissioned the building of these cabinets from James Frost, at a cost of £24 each.

***One of a pair of bow-fronted mahogany display cabinets*, by James Frost of Bakewell, *c.*1798**

F 71 Feldspar
Locality not recorded
G 77 Mica in calcareous spar
Locality not recorded
G 75 Kyanite and staurolite in schist
Locality not recorded
F 226 Sulphur and Gypsum
Locality not recorded
C 165 Sphalerite, galena, calcite and pyrite
Staunton Harold, Leicestershire
C 160 Galena, sphalerite and pyrite
Staunton Harold, Leicestershire
G 74 Kyanite and staurolite in schist
Locality not recorded
F 172 Silver
Schneeberg, Germany
F 188 Malachite
Locality not recorded
F 192 Haematite
Elba, France

Joshua Reynolds painted three generations of the Cavendish family, beginning with the third Duke. Some of his best portraits are of the Duchess Georgiana. This unfinished painting, with Georgiana emerging mysteriously from the bare canvas, was made in the early 1780s, when the sitter was in her twenties, just before the time of her ascent to public renown. Georgiana appears demure, with glowing pink cheeks and powdered hair tied back with ribbons, wearing a broad-brimmed black hat. Reynolds kept the picture in his studio until his death, evidently considering it one of his best and most original portraits. It was later given to Georgiana's son, the sixth Duke of Devonshire, by Mary Palmer, the artist's niece.

***Portrait of Georgiana, Duchess of Devonshire*, by Joshua Reynolds, 1780–81**

527
SIR JOSHUA REYNOLDS. 1723-1792
Georgiana, Duchess of Devonshire

During the winter of 1966/7 the future twelfth Duke, Stoker Cavendish, took his fiancée Amanda Heywood-Lonsdale to Cartier on Bond Street to choose an engagement ring. She selected this ring for its modern style, later learning that it had won a De Beers Diamonds International Award for design the previous year. Their engagement was announced in January 1967 and the wedding took place in June.

***Diamond ring*, by Cartier, 1960s**

This giant crystal of quartz was discovered on the Simplon Pass in Switzerland and acquired by the celebrated scientist Benjamin Thompson, also known as Count Rumford. He presented it to the Duchess Georgiana, along with a sample of porphyry broken from the highest point of Mount Saint Gothard, as she was travelling back through Switzerland, in August 1793. It was displayed alongside the enormous green gemstone known as Dom Pedro's Emerald, found in Colombia and acquired by the sixth Duke in the 1830s, at the Great Exhibition of 1851.

 Giant quartz crystal from the Simplon Pass

The brooch in the form of a dragonfly, one of a number in The Devonshire Collections representing insects, rests on *Flora luxurians; or, The Florist's Delight*, by James Sowerby, published in 1789.

 ***A gold, enamel and gem-set dragonfly brooch*, maker unknown, *c.*1900**

A veiled figure of a woman, one of the Vestal Virgins of ancient Rome, kneels and holds a dish of burning oil, symbolic of the eternal fire she attends at the altar in the Temple of Vesta, the Roman goddess of hearth and home. She wears the *suffibulum*, or white woollen veil, part of the traditional attire of the Vestals along with long white gowns symbolizing their purity, directly linked to the well-being of the Roman state. The Italian sculptor Raffaele Monti arrived in London in the 1840s, having been previously commissioned by the sixth Duke in Milan to create this statue; he was to make a successful career as a sculptor in Victorian Britain. The technique of carving marble to resemble transparent veils, for which Monti became known, looks back to the famous standing figure of the *Vestal Virgin Tuccia*, similarly swathed, carved by the Venetian sculptor Antonio Corradini in the eighteenth century, kept now at the Palazzo Barberini in Rome.

 ***A Veiled Vestal*, by Raffaele Monti, *c.*1846–7**

The upright forms and squared handles of this vase convey a feeling of antique grandeur, and indeed the peach-coloured marble from which it is made—occhio di pavone ('peacock's eye'), a limestone from Turkey—is extremely rare. One of a pair, it was made in Rome under the auspices of the sixth Duke's agent, Gaspare Gabrielli, and sent to London in 1820. The Duke also placed four stone columns in the Dome Room, two of the 'finest oriental alabaster'—in fact, a banded calcite probably mined in Italy—and the others of pavonazzetto (a brecciated, or fragmented, marble). The Duke salvaged them from the garden at Richmond House in London, where their wooden cases were 'half devoured by dry rot', as he wrote in his *Handbook*.

***One of a pair of occhio di pavone marble vases*, 1819**

The Ante-Library, part of the sixth Duke's North Wing, was a place to meet before dinner—'that most formal, weariest, hungriest moment of life less painful when the patients are squeezed together in a small compass', as the Duke wrote. William Cowen's watercolour, included in a specially bound copy, printed on large folio paper, of the sixth Duke's *Handbook*, shows one of the upright pair of occhio di pavone vases the Duke placed in the Dome Room, next to the Ante-Library, undoubtedly a topic of conversation at pre-dinner gatherings.

***Handbook of Chatsworth and Hardwick*, by William Cavendish, sixth Duke of Devonshire, 1845**

The Finnish craftsman Henrik Wigström was the head work-master at Fabergé from 1903, the year the world-famous jewellery-maker established a branch in London. English collectors were, in particular, fond of boxes decorated with views painted in enamel of famous buildings, which had been in vogue in Russia for over a hundred years. The Chatsworth box was made by Wigström alongside five others with views of royal palaces in Great Britain. It features Chatsworth on the cover and base in rose-coloured enamel, applied over oyster guilloché, a decorative technique in which an intricate repeating pattern is engraved using a machine lathe. It was given as a Christmas present by Queen Alexandra to the Dowager Duchess Louise, widow of the eighth Duke.

A Fabergé gold and guilloché enamel snuff-box, **by Henrik Immanuel Wigström, 1899–1908**

This is one of the earliest editions of the works of Roman poet Ovid, and includes his *Amores* and *Metamorphoses*. Edited by the humanist scholar Bonus Accursius, it was printed in Venice by the publisher Bernardinus Rizus in 1486–7. The annotations in sepia ink are in an unidentified sixteenth-century hand.

***Opera*, by Publius Ovidius Naso (known as Ovid), edited by Bonus Accursius, 1486–7**

Duchess Georgiana's poem recalling her perilous crossing of the Saint Gothard Pass in the autumn of 1793 was first published in 1802, in Paris, in English and French. Following her death another edition appeared, with lithographs of drawings by Lady Elizabeth Foster, who had accompanied Georgiana on her mountain journey. Foster's drawings are accomplished amateur views of the scenery, but appear conventional alongside the imaginative leaps taken by Georgiana's poem, with its references to geology, learned notes and allusions to the Swiss national hero, William Tell. *The Passage of the Mountain of Saint Gothard* was Georgiana's greatest literary work, all the more daring for being written at a time when women rarely published.

***The Passage of the Mountain of Saint Gothard*, by Georgiana, Duchess of Devonshire, *c.*1816**

Woodblock-printed and hand-painted wallpaper from China came into vogue in Britain in the mid-eighteenth century. It arrived on the ships of the East India Company, after having travelled from Canton (modern Guangzhou) to London.[12] Many of the designs showed flowers, plants and birds, and summoned up ideal Chinese gardens in the boudoirs and private spaces of rich houses. Four bedrooms at Chatsworth were decorated by the sixth Duke with Chinese wallpaper dating from 1790 to 1810, including the Wellington Bedroom, which appears in these photographs.

***Blocked and hand-painted Chinese wallpaper*, late eighteenth century**

Lady Anne Somerset, the daughter of the fourth Duke of Beaufort, was fourteen when the Swiss artist Jean-Étienne Liotard made this pastel portrait of her on a thin sheet of vellum. She wears a revealing floral-print dress provided by the artist, who brought back other decorative costumes from the Levant in which his female sitters posed. At the age of eighteen Lady Anne married the seventh Earl of Northampton in London, and gave birth to a daughter, Elizabeth, the following year. Shortly afterwards she accompanied her husband to Venice in his role as Ambassador Extraordinary; like him, she died of tuberculosis a few years later, at the age of twenty-two.[13] Although no records survive of the portrait having been drawn by Liotard, the meticulous detail, smoothness and sense of diffuse, slightly dulled light show the hand of the Swiss master. Lady Anne's daughter, Lady Elizabeth Compton, married Lord George Cavendish, the fifth Duke's younger brother and grandfather of the seventh Duke.

Portrait of Lady Anne Somerset, later Countess of Northampton, **by Jean-Étienne Liotard, *c.*1755**

The Carriages have never been dismantled at
the difficult places were carry'd by men with
ye aid of Cords.

Biova. The letter A Passage on ye side
of the Lake — 15 of August. [1793]
I shall begin an Itinerary. desired the
say any thing else. and draw how far it wd be
practicable to you & Harriet. before 9

Bellinzona 12th | We set out in the Evg — and our agreement was made at Bellinzona with Andreazzi the Inn keeper, who sends one
be fully trusted, civil & attentive young Men — who many
in Chairs with 3 or 4 guides to each — We set out
rough & my Sister had best have her own if
she finds them too rough — they are
Horses — The riding horses are strong between
but you shd have ye own saddles, as the
womans saddle is very bad & the Cu Cu
of saddle were & there are but 2.
we set out in the Evg & only get to Polleggio 4 hours — a decent Inn, good butter, & good fish from the Tesino, along whose banks we had been delighted with the most beautiful scenery only at last too much adorned by a violent Thunder & lightning Storm. — But the natural Stage is Giornico — by all accts very good — only 6 hours & makes the next day easier.

Polleggio 13th | We ascended the banks of the Tesino, the Road good & the bridges over the Cascades of the torrent beautiful. — We dined in a most beautiful spot at the Dazio grande a single excise house, but with a room as neat as any Inn in England. — excellent butter & fish & a very rare & good bird the name I have forgot.

Georgiana's long exile on the Continent in the early 1790s, when her husband sent her away for carrying the child of her lover, the future prime minister Charles Grey, was a time of freedom and happiness but also of painful absence from her three children, Georgiana, Harriet and William, the latter of whom was only ten months old when she left; her long poem *The Passage of the Mountain of Saint Gothard* was dedicated to them.

This fascinating letter was written by Georgiana to Countess Spencer, her mother, over several days in August 1793, as she made her return journey over the Saint Gothard Pass—the leg of her trip back up through Italy to France, which resulted in her poem. Georgiana's party, including her sister Harriet and her daughter Caroline, Lady Elizabeth Foster, guides and servants, set off from Bellinzona, in the Swiss Alps, on Monday, 12 August, travelling at first on litter chairs 'slung between horses', and following the course of the River Ticino up the valley to Airolo, on the southern slopes of the Saint Gothard Mountains. They dined well on fresh fish and 'a very rare & good bird the name I have forgot', and also butter, which Georgiana mentions several times. As the gentle ascent began from Airolo, they exchanged the litter chairs for the saddle, but the rough path obliged them to ride '*en homme*', rather than side-saddle. Georgiana's descriptions show her appreciation of the wild scenery: 'The Tesino falls in cascades—great blocks of snow lie in parts like blocks of marble.' At the top of the mountain they were welcomed by a Capuchin monk, who provided them with excellent cheese, and butter 'the best I ever tasted'.

As they passed down the mountain, they were obliged to travel through a foot tunnel towards the Devil's Bridge: 'here our expectations of Grandeur & horror were alone justified', although they found the bridge itself disappointingly easy to cross. At Altdorf they marvelled at the statues of William Tell '& the other authors of Swiss liberty', in preparation for their arrival at Lake Lucerne, where the sight of the William Tell Chapel, marking the spot where Tell leapt from his captor's boat in a storm, inspired the climax of Georgiana's poem:

And hail the chapel! hail the platform wild!
    Where *Tell* directed the avenging dart,
With well-strung arm, that first preserv'd his child,
    Then wing'd the arrow to the tyrant's heart.

Her eye always on practical matters, Georgiana also wondered about a carriage-sharing scheme for travelling aristocrats, given that it was impracticable to take a carriage over the mountains. If you were returning to England, and another family was heading down to Italy, could you not leave your carriage for them at Pesto, on the Italian side, and they theirs for you at Lucerne?

***Letter from Georgiana, Duchess of Devonshire to Countess Spencer*, 15 August 1793**

The subject, Lady Caroline Lamb, a niece of Georgiana Cavendish, was a writer known for her Gothic novel *Glenarvon*, which offered a satirical portrait of Lord Byron, her former lover. This miniature was painted by Emma Eleonora Kendrick, a portraitist who had been appointed miniature painter to King William IV in 1831, a year after she published her book *Conversations on the Art of Miniature Painting*. Sometime before painting this image, Kendrick made a three-quarter-length miniature watercolour portrait of Lady Caroline, holding a book and looking pensive. (It is now in the Victoria and Albert Museum.) Around the same time, Lady Caroline had taken, without permission, a portrait of Byron from the house of the publisher John Murray. Before it was returned to Murray, she had Kendrick make a copy and set it in a locket inscribed with the words *Ne crede Byron*—'Trust not in Byron.' The bullet lodged in the table, incidentally, is a stray round from soldiers training behind the house during the Second World War.

***Portrait miniature of Lady Caroline Lamb*, by Emma Eleonora Kendrick, *c.*1810**

 Coronet from the Devonshire Parure, by C. F. Hancock, 1856 (see page 197)

The Devonshire Parure was one of the sixth Duke's most audacious interventions in the family collection. It was created for the Countess Granville, the wife of the sixth Duke's nephew, who, with her husband, was to attend the coronation of Tsar Alexander in Moscow in 1856. Remembering the extravagance of the Russian Court at the imperial coronation of 1826, which he had attended, the sixth Duke realized that the Countess could not possibly attend without spectacular jewels to rival those worn by the Russian aristocratic women. English women, it is said, dreaded these festivities, fearing their inability to match the splendour of the Russian Court. The Devonshire Collections held perfect raw material for such a jewellery set: the antique gems collected in the early part of the 1700s. These gems, which, since the time of the second Duke, had been kept in the Plate Room at Devonshire House, were an essential part of a gentleman's scholarly library, alongside prints, books, drawings and other works of art.[14] Some dated from the first centuries of the era before Christ, while others were cut in Italy during the sixteenth century. The Devonshire collection of gems, only a small number of which were plundered for the Parure, also contains English royal portraits, some attributed to the gem-engraver Richard Astyll; these include two cameo portraits of Elizabeth I, one of Edward VI as a child and a sardonyx cameo of Henry VIII with his three children.

The sixth Duke ordered, from the London jeweller C. F. Hancock, eighty-eight of these precious stones, otherwise worthy of the greatest museum of antiquities, to be mounted in seven elaborate ornaments, like sparkling armour: a diadem, comb, bandeau, coronet, necklace, stomacher and bracelet. Hancock's masterpiece of Victorian goldsmith's work was inspired by sixteenth-century Tudor jewellery. He surrounded the frames with diamonds, 'to lighten it up', as Hancock wrote in a letter to Joseph Paxton (they were later removed by the wife of the eighth Duke and, later still, replaced by paste gems). The most celebrated of all, a cornelian intaglio carved by Dioskourides, the gem-engraver to Alexander the Great, was set in the bandeau. It shows the Greek warrior Diomedes, who, during the sacking of Troy, stole a sacred statue of the goddess Athena that supposedly protected Troy—he is portrayed in mind-boggling miniature, clambering over the altar of Apollo and holding the statue, known as the Palladion. The large blue stone at the centre of the coronet is a lapis lazuli carved with the image of Hercules, wearing the skin of the Nemean Lion. Around the image of the Emperor Tiberius, carved in sardonyx and set in the necklace, an inscription in Kufic shows that it was once owned by a Mamluk prince from the fourteenth century.

***Stomacher from the Devonshire Parure*, by C. F. Hancock, 1856**

Diadem from the Devonshire Parure (detail), by C. F. Hancock, 1856 (see page 197)

 Bandeau from the Devonshire Parure (detail), by C. F. Hancock, 1856 (see page 197)

Diadem from the Devonshire Parure, by C. F. Hancock, 1856 (see page 197)

The sixth Duke inherited his fondness for mastiffs from his father, the fifth Duke, whose love of dogs was such that he was nicknamed 'Canis'. This is the collar of leather and silver made in 1832 by Robert Garrard for the sixth Duke's mastiff, Hector, whose name is inscribed on the key.

***Collar for Hector*, by Robert Garrard, 1832**

Henry Tonks's early career as a surgeon put him in good stead when it came to drawing and painting the human figure, although he was also one of the first British artists to paint in a style influenced by French artists such as Renoir and Monet. A contemporary wrote of paintings such as *The Strolling Players*—showing a group of actors practising a scene in the living room of a boarding house—that Tonks's principal subject was 'the interpretation of young womanhood, surprised by us in some wistful reverie'.[15] The model who sat for this small study of a girl's head, acquired by the eleventh Duke, was also used for the right-hand figure in *The Strolling Players*, although Tonks has adjusted her pose for the final painting. Her identity remains a mystery.

***Girl's head (Study for The Strolling Players)*, by Henry Tonks, *c.*1906**

AVCTORI.

M.Varrõe.Celio.Galba.C.Ictio Mu tiano.Cor.Nipote.L.Piſone.Tubero ne.Seneca.Fabio Veſtale.Annio Feci ale.Fabião.Catõe Ceſorio . Vitruuio.

EXTERNI.

Theophraſto.Praxitele.Iuba Re.Ni candro.Sotaco.Sudine.Alexãdro Po lyhiſtore.Apione.Pliſtonico.Duricle. Herodoto.Euemero.Ariſtagora. Dio nyſio.Artẽidoro.Bucorida. Antiſthe ne.Democrito.Demotele.Lycea.

LIBRO.XXXVII.CONTIENE lorigine delle gemme.

Gẽma di Polycrate Tyranno & di Pyr rho Re:& quali fuſſino optimi ſculp tori:& quali opere nobili:& chi prima aRõa hebbe la dactilotheca. Ca.i.

Gemme portate nel triompho di Põ peo:& natura di Criſtallo & medicĩa: & quãdo fu trouato la Myrrina & del luxo circa queſte : & natã della Myrri na.& quello che glauctori hanno men tito dellambra. Ca.ii.

Naſcimẽto medicine & generationi dAambra . Item Lyncurio pietra & ſue medicine. Ca.iii.

Diamanti & ſue ſpetie & medicine. Item Perle. Ca.iiii.

Smeraldi di piu ragioni & pietre uer di tranſparenti. Ca.v.

Spetie & uitii di pietra Opolo:& ex perimenti & uarie gemme. Ca.vi.

Spetie uarie di Carbonchi & loro ui tii & expimẽti & gẽme ardẽti. Ca.vii.

Topatii & Callaite & gemme uerdi non tranſparenti. Ca.viii.

Iaſpidi di uarie ſpetie. Ca.ix.

Piu gemme per alphabeto. Ca.x.

Gẽme nomĩate da mẽbri hũani & da animali & da altre choſe. Ca.xi.

Gemme che choſi naſcano & gẽme facte & figure di gemme. Ca.xii.

Modo in prouare le gemme. Ca.xiii.

Soma choſe hiſtorie & obſeruationi. M.ccc.

AVCTORI.

M.Varrone.Acti de triomphi. Mecẽ nate.Iaccho. Cornelio.Boccho.

EXTERNI.

Iuba Re.Xenocrate di Zenone.Sudi ne.Eſchilo.Philoxene.Euripide.Nicã dro.Satyro.Theophraſto.Carete.Phi lomene.Dẽocrate.Xenotino . Metro doro.Sotaco.Pythea. Timeo Siculo. Nicea.Theocreſto.Aſaruba . Naſea. Cteomene. Cteſea . Mithridate . So phocle:Archelao Re.Calliſtrato.Dẽo crito.Iſmemo.Olympico. Alexandro Polyhiſtore.Apione.Ori. Zoroaſtre. Zactalia.

The French printer Nicolas Jenson was one of the leading publishers in Venice in the 1470s, during the first great era of printing in the city, and was known for his beautifully designed volumes with their clear Roman fonts. Pliny the Elder's *Historia naturalis* was left unfinished at the author's death in AD 79 in the eruption of Vesuvius, but it remained the most compendious source of knowledge for the sciences and learning of the ancient world for centuries to come. This edition, an Italian translation made by the famed humanist Cristoforo Landino, is unusual for being decorated with miniature paintings, like an illuminated manuscript, by a highly talented unknown artist. Peacocks, a leopard, a squirrel, stags and other creatures populate an inlaid marble altar on this page, an index to Chapter 37, on the origin and nature of gems and precious stones, also listing Pliny's sources—the Classical authors he drew on for his book.

Four eagles support the feet of these weighty tureens, the handles in the form of two larger eagles grasping oak branches with leaves and acorns. They were the largest pieces made by the London silversmith Paul Storr, and would have been an imposing presence in the sixth Duke's Great Dining Room, the Rococo forms creating a contrast with the more Classically inspired candelabras, also made by Storr for the sixth Duke.

One of a pair of soup tureens and covers, by Paul Storr, 1820–21

Benjamin Vulliamy was the son of a Swiss clock-maker who settled in London. In 1773 he became clock-maker to King George III. He was best known for the style of his mantel clocks: Derby porcelain was distinctively combined with gilt metal, and the timepiece set in a sculptural vignette. In this elaborate clock, more like a little piece of sculpture, a porcelain putto peers up at the clock dial, set in a half-column, while a set-square, mallet, chisel and books are scattered on marble steps at the column's base, along with a scroll bearing the motto *Fugit irreparabile tempus*, a line from Virgil: 'Irrecoverable time flies away.' Georgiana, Duchess of Devonshire, bought the clock from Vulliamy, probably in November 1787.

A mantel clock **(detail), by Benjamin Vulliamy Snr, *c.*1787**

SCENE V

CURIOSITY IN ARCADIA

Delving back in time again, now to 1759. The scenery around Chatsworth is changing, such that if you had fallen asleep in one of the bedrooms in 1750, and woken ten years later, you might think on looking out of the window that the house had been uprooted and transported to somewhere far, far away. A small army of labourers works tirelessly, moving earth, shaping, flattening, creating new contours and vistas. To the west, thick hedges and stone walls are being torn down, while swathes of land are being drained, ploughed and planted with vast quantities of grass seed. Over eighty varieties of tree and shrub have arrived from Philadelphia, including the swamp viburnum (*Viburnum nudum*), the tulip tree (*Liriodendron tulipifera*) and the honey locust (*Gleditsia triacanthos*), ready to be spread around the garden and park. Ten thousand oaks have been planted, fifteen thousand mountain ash and birch, and more than seventy thousand thorn trees, many on the slope rising behind the house, others to the south, beyond the Canal Pond, towards the hamlet of Calton Lees. WILLIAM CAVENDISH, the fourth Duke of Devonshire, is bringing to completion the work begun by his father, heralding a new era of 'naturalness' in the life of Chatsworth, with the landscape transformed into the very image of rural ease.

Credit for the transformation of Chatsworth's setting is often assigned to the landscape gardener Lancelot 'Capability' Brown, who was engaged by the fourth Duke of Devonshire in 1758; and yet these changes had already been under way in the 1720s and 1730s. The third Duke changed much of the formal garden created by his grandfather. Statues were removed; structures such as

Design for a cascade at Chatsworth, by William Kent, *c.*1743–8

the Bowling Green House and the Ice House were repositioned next to the Canal Pond; ponds were filled in; terraced formal gardens were replaced by sloping lawns. Trees were felled—2,340 in 1732, according to accounts—and planted in their thousands, changing the appearance of the countryside.[1] It was a new 'look' for parks that was being promoted by the leading designers of the time, including William Kent and his patron, the architect Richard Boyle, the third Earl of Burlington. Kent visited Chatsworth in the 1730s and made drawings showing fantastical gardens, never realized but fully in the spirit of the times. His ideal garden was irregular, informal and full of surprises, based not on a single, centralized point of view but on assembling a collection of viewpoints. It was an aesthetic statement, but also a political one: a metaphor for the new parliamentary system formed to balance the power of the King in the wake of the 'Glorious Revolution'.

The fourth Duke, with the help of Lancelot Brown and his foreman Michael Millican, continued his father's radical decluttering, with the aim of creating 'natural'-looking scenery, without affectation, that was nonetheless subject to the practical needs of the house. This meant moving working aspects of the estate, such as orchards, farmyards and kitchen gardens; and, in 1758, getting rid of the rabbit warren—rabbit skins had formed part of the estate finances for over two hundred years.[2] Brown's designs for the garden framed an Arcadian setting of aristocratic elegance, comfort and repose. Many of his changes can still be seen today: clumps of trees positioned for an artless, 'rustic' effect, planted on cultivated meadows and artificial hills. The previous Duke had already created pleasure grounds in which sheep grazed, tended by the head shepherd, Sam Furness, and his boys—workers on the estate but also actors on an Arcadian stage. The river itself was made to play a role, widened to appear more prominent, and given a new crossing, the Three Arch Bridge; built by the architect James Paine and finished in 1761, it was positioned at a forty-five-degree angle to the house and afforded the best views on arrival

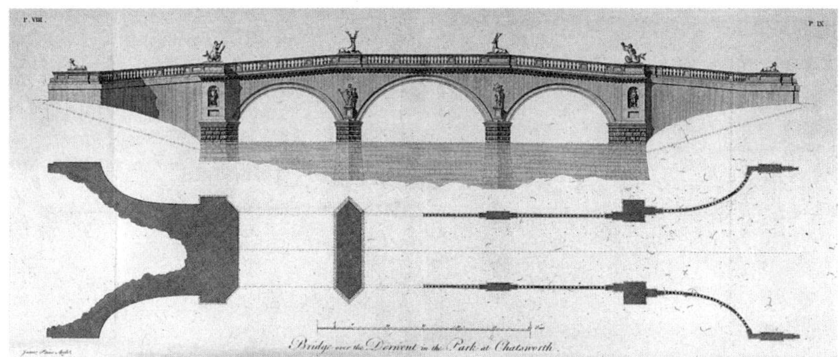

Design for the Three Arch Bridge, from Plans, Elevations and Sections, of Noblemen and Gentlemen's Houses, by James Paine, 1767

and departure. In addition to the smaller One Arch Bridge and the handsomely proportioned Water Mill alongside the river, Paine also designed, to the north-east of the house, the new Stable Block, a boldly rusticated quadrangle that emanated solidity and weight.[3]

The startling new landscape at Chatsworth, with its wide-open views, made a great impression on Horace Walpole when he arrived by post-chaise in the summer of 1760. Walpole, a politician, aesthete and collector, who designed his own villa, Strawberry Hill, in the Gothic style, was on his annual peregrination around country houses, which he would scour from cellar to attic, exhausting housekeepers with his never-ending demands and insatiable curiosity. The light-filled classicism of Chatsworth was entirely different from the shadowy mystery and medievalism of Strawberry Hill, yet he could not help but be impressed by the 'richness and vivacity of prospect' of the fourth Duke's house.[4] 'It is a glorious situation; the vale rich in corn and verdure, vast woods hang down the hills, which are green to the top, and the immense rocks only serve to dignify the prospect. The river runs before the door, and serpentizes more than you can conceive in the vale.'[5]

The fourth Duke's contributions to the family's art collection were few, but not without significance. One of the most charming paintings in the collection was painted by Johan Zoffany, showing the Cavendish children playing in the gardens at Chiswick, a work completed a year after the Duke's death in 1764. His father, the third Duke, had also made some eye-catching contributions, including the painting by Rembrandt traditionally identified as a portrait of King Uzziah of Judah, which he bought in 1742, as well as one of Van Dyck's most celebrated portraits, that of the lawyer and politician Arthur Goodwin, given to him by the prime minister, Sir Robert Walpole.

Portrait of Lord Burlington and Family,
by Jean-Baptiste van Loo, 1739

But it was through marriage that the fourth Duke made his most lasting contribution to The Devonshire Collections. When he came to the dukedom in 1755, he was newly widowed after the loss of his wife, Charlotte. She had been the only surviving child of Richard Boyle, the third Earl of Burlington, the 'architect earl' who was the great champion of the Palladian style of building in England. Lady Charlotte was the sole heiress of the Burlington estates, which ultimately passed to her offspring: among them were two grand houses her father had built, Chiswick House, to the west of London, and Burlington House on Piccadilly, as well as Bolton Abbey in Yorkshire and the romantic castle of Lismore in Ireland. (It was at Lismore—which, incidentally, neither Charlotte nor her father ever visited—that the important medieval Gaelic manuscript now known as the Book of Lismore was discovered during the early years of the nineteenth century; it was donated to University College, Cork, by the twelfth Duke of Devonshire in 2020.) Chiswick was designed to house Burlington's collection of art and books; among the paintings in his collection were portraits by Rembrandt, Frans Hals and Velázquez; the *Donne Triptych* by Hans Memling; and paintings by Sebastiano Ricci—all Old Masters that signalled his status as a leading connoisseur and taste-maker of his time. Indeed, the poet Alexander Pope addressed his famous 'epistle', 'Of Taste', to Burlington; this influential poem argued for a new era of taste in Britain, one that rejected the overheated Baroque then prevalent in architecture and landscape design in favour of Classical order and rational good sense.

The buildings of the Venetian architect Andrea Palladio were Burlington's greatest love—he had fallen for them during his tours of Italy in 1715 and 1719, and bought the architect's drawings by the dozen, some in Italy, others in Paris from the collection of John Talman (the son of William Talman, the architect who rebuilt Chatsworth from 1686 to 1696).[6] Lord Burlington was largely responsible for the eighteenth-century craze

A View of Chatsworth,
by William Marlow, *c*.1770

for Palladian architecture, an austerely Classical Roman style that contrasted with the decadent excesses of the Baroque. The culmination of Burlington's Palladian enthusiasm was Chiswick House, the compact, cubic design of which was inspired by Palladio's buildings in the Veneto. From John Talman, Burlington also bought many drawings by the English Palladian artist and architect Inigo Jones, including his designs for masques at the Stuart Courts of James I and Charles I, and his annotated copy of *De architectura*, the celebrated work by the Roman architect Vitruvius. Burlington commissioned marble busts of Jones and Palladio from the sculptor John Michael Rysbrack—images of his two heroes that were to be given pride of place at Chiswick, itself a monument to Palladianism.

The Boyles were a creative family, a natural match for the art-loving Cavendishes. The French artist Jean-Baptiste van Loo's portrait of Burlington and his family shows the Earl and his wife, Countess Dorothy, their elegantly attired servant James Cambridge behind, and their daughters Dorothy and Charlotte, 'all disposed in the Virtuosi way', as George Vertue put it.[7] (*Virtuosi* was the word used to describe the art lovers of the day.) Charlotte points to an open book of music on her mother's lap, who in turn holds an oil-paint palette. The Countess was a talented amateur artist, who received lessons in painting and drawing from William Kent (although he was a much better designer of furniture and interiors than he was a painter).[8] Horace Walpole, in his *Anecdotes of Painting in England*, praised her talent for 'likenesses' and 'caricatura'.[9]

In the light of this vast inheritance from his wife's family—of great works of art, buildings and estates, as well as family memorabilia—the fourth Duke hardly needed to collect art himself—and he hardly had time, as it happened, for he died in the Netherlands at the age of forty-four, the result of a weak constitution.

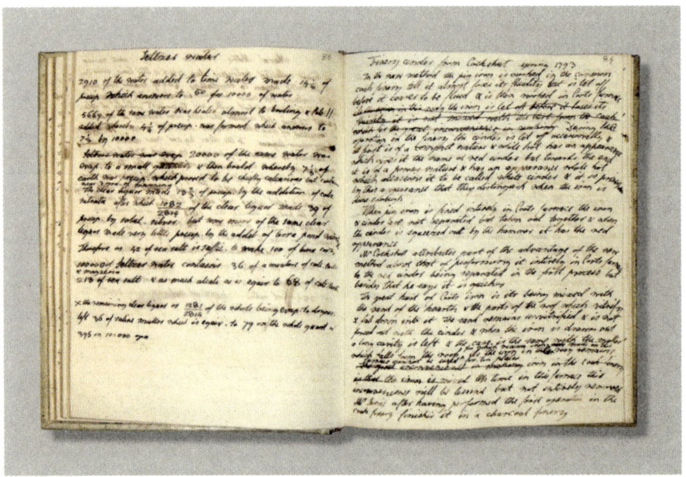

White Book No. 1,
by Henry Cavendish, 1786–99

The fourth Duke's major legacy was the glorious new landscape setting for Chatsworth. His son, the fifth Duke, added to The Devonshire Collections according to the taste of the time—elegant French snuffboxes and gilded furniture—but is largely remembered for the drama surrounding his marriage to Georgiana. It was through the contrasting figure of the fourth Duke's cousin, the natural scientist Henry Cavendish, that an entirely different legacy was passed to Chatsworth.

Henry Cavendish was one of the great and most prolific experimental physicists of his age. 'It may be said of him,' wrote his fellow scientist Humphry Davy after Henry's death in 1810, 'that whatever he has done had been perfect at the moment of its production… Since the death of Newton… England has sustained no scientific loss so great as that of Cavendish.'[10] He was tall and thin; he wore an outmoded violet suit and periwig, and a three-cornered hat, the bold effect of which was somewhat diminished by his squeaky voice, shuffling gait and excruciating timidity. His life was almost wholly without active incident, except, it is said, for the time that he saved a woman from an enraged cow on Clapham Common.[11]

From his father (the second Duke's son), Lord Charles, also a scientist, Henry inherited an obsession for precision, which became the basis for his successful and ground-breaking experiments; among his interests were the chemistry of 'airs', or gases of specific density, and waters; and the law governing the electrical forces of attraction and repulsion. He designed and commissioned scientific instruments, less with a view to their impressive appearance, as was common, than to their ruthless effectiveness in measuring to the finest degree. These instruments assisted numerous discoveries: the nature, for example, of the electric charge produced by the torpedo fish, and, as a result, the nature of electrical charges and voltage. He discovered the element that was to become known as hydrogen. He developed a mechanical theory of heat that was a precursor to one of the theories of thermodynamics,

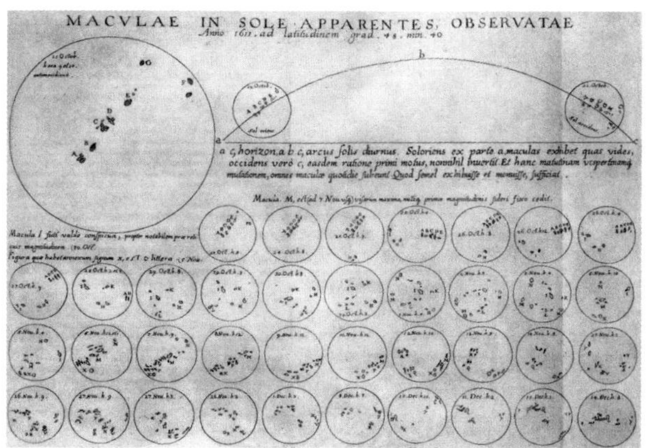

Istoria e dimostrazioni intorno alle macchie solari,
by Galileo Galilei, 1613

noting it down and moving to the next problem, not bothering to publish it, so that only later did its significance become apparent. Most famously, working at his house in Clapham, he was able to calculate accurately the mean density (and, by extension, the mean weight) of the Earth.

Cavendish also conducted experiments in mineralogy and geology; he belonged to a group that met to discuss such questions at the Cat and Bagpipes, a pub on the corner of Downing Street. He made copious notes on mineral samples in a vellum-bound book, known as the White Book, the only notebook of his known to survive, now kept at Chatsworth.

He rarely travelled, but when he did it was for the purposes of fieldwork. His tours of Britain, in a horse-drawn carriage with his assistant Charles Blagden, were driven by a deep curiosity about the changing landscape in the early days of the Industrial Revolution. When not measuring the heights of mountains, they were conversing with James Watt in Birmingham about his revolutionary steam engine, visiting ironworks in Merthyr and Coalbrookdale, observing quarrying, coke-making, tin-plating, milling, hammering and smelting. At Chesterfield they suffered a highly uncomfortable descent into a mine, and at Sheffield, according to Blagden, stayed at 'vile' lodgings, the Fortune Inn.[12] Such discomfort was simply part of the experience at a time when experimental science meant travelling out and seeing the world, whether up a volcano or down a mine.

Cavendish's influential legacy has survived in several forms. In 1783, at Bedford Square, he established a 'semi-private' library open to learned guests (he himself always left a receipt when 'borrowing' a book from his own library). This library, the bulk of his scientific papers and a small number of scientific instruments found their way into The Devonshire Collections, and are kept at Chatsworth (they were inherited by the sixth Duke through his grandfather Lord George Cavendish). The seventh Duke provided funds for a laboratory of experimental science at the University of Cambridge that would bear his

Metamorphosis insectorum Surinamensium,
by Maria Merian, 1705

ancestor's name; and from 1874 to 1879 James Clerk Maxwell (who developed electromagnetic theory and created the famous thermodynamic thought experiment 'Maxwell's Demon') edited Cavendish's electrical papers for publication, revealing that Cavendish had achieved important experimental results that were credited to other scientists—thus establishing an undeniable place of prominence for Cavendish in the history of science.

When Cavendish's library arrived at Chatsworth, the books, numbering some twelve thousand, were gradually arranged by Hart, after his new Library was finished in 1830. Alongside early editions of books by Nicolaus Copernicus and Galileo Galilei were the first modern atlas, the *Theatrum orbis terrarum*, by Abraham Ortell, from 1570; Maria Merian's stunning illustrated volume of natural history, *Metamorphosis insectorum Surinamensium* of 1705; and many books on travel and large, illustrated books on natural history, all marked with Cavendish's distinctive ink stamp.

They were stored initially in the Oak Room, and must have taken up most of the wall space in this small, low-ceilinged chamber. They eventually took their place in the sixth Duke's Library alongside the architectural volumes that arrived with the library of Lord Burlington, the Greek and Latin texts acquired by the fifth Duke, as well as the books collected by his ancestors—the manuscripts and libraries of the Earls of Devonshire, and of the first great collectors in the family, the first and second Dukes. Although the first Duke might have been surprised that a whole room could be devoted to storing and showing books, spine outwards (in his day you lodged books wherever, and however, they would fit), he would have understood the importance of the Library as it appeared in the sixth Duke's time, the multifarious, magnetic centre of the collections at Chatsworth.

 Playing card, inscribed on reverse by Lady Charlotte Boyle, *c.*1747 (see page 222)

Lady Charlotte Boyle desires her Compliments to Lord Hartington & begs the favour the honour the pleasure & the comfort of a little Claret. It is a charming lover's note, inscribed on the back of a nine of hearts playing card, from Lady Charlotte Boyle to William Cavendish, the future fourth Duke of Devonshire. Their marriage in the spring of 1748 had been arranged since their childhood, and was a dynastic alliance that brought the vast inheritance of Richard Boyle, third Earl of Burlington, including large estates, London properties, and a considerable art collection, into Devonshire hands. Against these odds the marriage was a happy one, as this playing card note suggests. It was also short, Charlotte Boyle dying six years (and four children) later, in 1754, the year before William became the fourth Duke.

***Playing card*, inscribed on reverse by Lady Charlotte Boyle, *c.*1747**

An owl perches atop this silver-gilt cup, a reference to the crest of the Savile family, for whom it was made. The elaborate design, known as 'auricular' after its resemblance to the folds of the ear, originated in Germany at the beginning of the 1600s. The maker of the cup, and other objects with the maker's mark of a hound sejant (seated dog), was a mystery for years, only recently confirmed as being Richard Blackwell II, master of one of the largest goldsmith's workshops in London.[13] It was inherited by the fifth Duke of Devonshire from his grandmother, Lady Dorothy Savile.

***The Savile cup and cover*, by Richard Blackwell II, *c.*1650**

Soldani was the last in a line of great Florentine sculptors in bronze, reaching back to Lorenzo Ghiberti in the fifteenth century. He was known for his copies in bronze of antique sculpture, as well as more recent works by Michelangelo, Sansovino and Bernini. Displayed here in the lavishly decorated State Music Room, its walls covered with stamped and gilded leather, *Virtue Triumphant over Vice*—an allegory of the triumph of Florence over Pisa—is a version of a famous work by the Flemish sculptor Giambologna.

***Virtue Triumphant over Vice*, by Massimiliano Soldani Benzi, early eighteenth century**

The Flemish sculptor John Michael Rysbrack based his white marble bust of the architect Inigo Jones, who had died seventy years earlier, on a famous drawing by Anthony van Dyck, also in the collection at Chatsworth. Van Dyck had captured Jones's quizzical expression and slightly awkward demeanour, and Rysbrack in turn preserves them in this bust. It was Inigo Jones who first introduced the Palladian style into English architecture, and Richard Boyle, the third Earl of Burlington, who popularized it through his designs for a number of major building projects. Rysbrack also made a bust of Palladio, giving Jones and the Italian architect matching outfits to show the connection between the two figures so venerated by Richard Boyle.

***Bust of Inigo Jones*, by John Michael Rysbrack, *c.*1725**

This fiery figure was drawn by Inigo Jones as a costume design for Thomas Campion's *The Lords' Maske*, one of the Court entertainments designed by Jones for James I and his consort, Queen Anne of Denmark—in this case to celebrate the marriage of James's daughter Elizabeth to Frederick, the Elector Palatine. Masques were elaborate stagings involving music, dance and spectacular sets, the men and women of the Court taking on costumed roles in what was essentially a ritual devoted to the glory of the reigning monarch. *The Lords' Maske* begins with Orpheus and Prometheus in a woodland, accompanied by music and song, over which eight bright stars moved 'in an exceeding strange and delightful manner', as Campion wrote in the published account of the play. He praises Inigo Jones's work as designer: 'I suppose fewe have ever seene more neate artifice, than Master Innigoe Jones shewed in contriving their Motion, who in all the rest of the workmanship which belong'd to the whole invention, shewed extraordinarie industrie and skill.'[14] Prometheus calls forth sixteen 'fiery spirits', in costumes designed by Inigo Jones: 'all their attires being alike composed of flames, with fierie Wings and Bases, bearing in either hand a Torch of Virgine Waxe', who enter and perform a courtly dance.

Jones was famed in his day for his designs for masques in his brilliant and fluid style of drawing, many of them conceived in collaboration with the poet Ben Jonson. His use of mechanics and technology to create spectacular effects drew on Italian theatre, which in Jones's hands were like the great Baroque ceiling paintings of palaces and churches come to life. For *The Lords' Maske*, Jones devised a rotating stage known as a *machina versatilis*; for another masque, he created the effect of a huge obelisk being pulled along the stage by a single golden thread.[15] Some 450 of his drawings for stage designs survive in the collection at Chatsworth, including those for set designs, proscenium arches and the elegant costumes of masquers, as well as for the more grotesque, comical costumes of characters known as anti-masquers.

The Lords' Maske was staged in the old Banqueting House at Whitehall, alongside a performance of *The Tempest* by William Shakespeare (first performed two years earlier), which itself includes masque-like scenes. Such elaborate entertainments needed a grander setting, however, and some years later James I commissioned Jones to build a larger, more extravagant Banqueting House. Jones drew on the Classical style of architecture he had seen on his tour of Italy in 1613 in the company of the Earl of Arundel. His 'Italian Sketchbook', also at Chatsworth, is full of drawings of ancient buildings and sculpture; and, in the Banqueting House, he produced one of the first truly Palladian buildings in England, still admired today, and one of the reasons that Jones is remembered more as an architect than as a stage designer.

***Torchbearer: A Fiery Spirit*, by Inigo Jones, 1613**

This splendid metal bird is called the 'Kniphausen' Hawk after the person for whom it was made: Georg Wilhelm von Kniphausen, Count of the Holy Roman Empire, Lord of Nienoort (today in the eastern Netherlands) and of the territory of Vredewold. It was a symbol of Georg Wilhelm's pride in his position and titles (he had them inscribed in capital letters on the beaker), and would have been prominently displayed in his lavishly decorated castle. On great occasions it might have been used as a pouring vessel—the head can be removed, and liquid poured through a hole in the bird's mouth. It is called the Kniphausen 'Hawk' as a matter of pure error, for the form of the bird encased in painted enamels and set with precious and semi-precious stones—a plethora of red garnets, amethysts, turquoises, emeralds, citrines, blue sapphires and three onyx cameos—is clearly that of an eagle.

The Kniphausen Hawk, 1697

Samuel Watson originally carved no fewer than fourteen martial trophies—concatenations of weapons and the appurtenances of war, arranged in a hanging shield-like arrangement—for the first Duke's Inner Court. They might have reminded the first Duke of his own role in the 'Glorious Revolution', in which the Catholic King James II was deposed and his Protestant daughter Mary, and her Dutch husband, William of Orange, were put in his place on the English throne. Only four of the trophies remain today, those on the east wall; it is not certain exactly when the trophies and other architectural decorations of the Inner Court were removed, but most probably during the nineteenth century.

***Martial trophies*, by Samuel Watson, 1690s**

This book contains architectural drawings by Samuel Watson that correspond with many of his carvings in wood, stone, marble and alabaster at Chatsworth. Shown here are designs for the inscription on the West Front. The bound miscellany of designs and documents also includes profile drawings of family members, made by Watson's grandson, the geologist White Watson, including one of his father, also called Samuel, 'Taken by the strength of memory', three years after his death. No images survive of Samuel Watson the elder—a portrait of him by James Thornhill, which was at one time in the possession of White Watson, has unfortunately been lost.

According to the biographical details Albin provides in his 1720 volume *A Natural History of English Insects*, he was born in Jamaica, and lived in Piccadilly, London, with his family—he trained one of his daughters, Elizabeth, as a watercolourist to aid him in his work. Albin was established as a teacher of watercolour painting before turning to natural history, one of his first commissions being from a Mrs How to paint 'a great Number of both *caterpillars* and *flies*'.[16] All the specimens illustrated in his volumes were painted from life, as he was keen to point out, although they often show the influence of the German-born illustrator Maria Sibylla Merian. His *A Natural History of Spiders* describes two hundred specimens, and includes three supplements: 'Of the Tarantula' by Dr Mead; and, by the 'late ingenious Dr Hooke', 'Microscopical Observations on the Carter Spider, and Jumping Spider' and 'Observations on the Flea, and Louse'.

***A Natural History of Spiders, and Other Curious Insects*, by Eleazar Albin, 1736**

Robert Hooke was a natural philosopher who trained first, briefly, as a painter, in the studio of Sir Peter Lely. Shortly afterwards, in the 1650s, he studied science at Oxford, and was thereafter appointed 'curator of experiments' at the newly founded Royal Society of London. His most famous book, *Micrographia*, was the first in the field of microscopy, and brought together a wide range of observations, recorded in drawings that he had presented to meetings of the Royal Society in 1663. The subjects include crystals, petrified wood, fossils, man-made objects such as the point of a needle, astronomical bodies, and, perhaps most famously of all, insects, in particular the flea, gnat and the louse (pictured here), shown in large, fold-out, copperplate engravings. Hooke was continuing work begun by Sir Christopher Wren, who had made drawings of insects seen through microscopes since the early 1650s.

***Micrographia; or, Some Physiological Descriptions of Minute Bodies Made by Magnifying Glasses, with Observations and Inquiries Thereupon*, by Robert Hooke, 1665**

This mahogany hall chair, with its simple foursquare proportions, somehow both proud and witty, looks at first sight like a piece of recycled architecture. It belongs to a set of twelve designed in the middle of the 1730s by William Kent for Chiswick House. For the architect of Chiswick, Richard Boyle, third Earl of Burlington, the triangular pediment backing and decoration, including acanthus and fish-scale patterns, were an advertisement for the Palladian building style he had popularized in England. William Kent's genius was in repurposing the forms of architecture to create a chair that seems itself like a little temple.

***Hall chair for Chiswick House*, by William Kent, *c.*1735**

Assembled from odd scraps of recycled plywood, the *Kröller-Müller Chair* has a rough-and-ready, cobbled-together feel quite unlike any other piece of furniture at Chatsworth. The designer, Piet Hein Eek, is known for his repurposing and recycling of disused materials. He originally made the chair in 2002 for a shed in the grounds of the Kröller-Müller Museum in Otterlo. It was so popular that he began collecting scraps of wood to create an edition of the chair, which first appeared a decade later.

***Kröller-Müller Chair*, by Piet Hein Eek, 2012**

INSIGNE SVM IERONYMI
CASII

Although his identity was for many years lost, the sitter in this portrait has been identified as the poet Girolamo Casio, a friend of the artist, by the initials 'C. B.' embroidered on his jacket—standing for 'Cassius Bononiensis', referring to his hometown of Bologna. His flowing, golden-brown locks, large limpid eyes and rich clothing show him to be a beautiful, well-heeled youth, although two other portraits of Casio made around the same time portray him with more worldly, ordinary features and a thick mop of hair. Boltraffio trained in Milan at the workshop of Leonardo da Vinci, and this is an idealized portrait very much in the style of that Renaissance master. On the reverse side of the panel a jawless skull rests in a darkened niche with an inscription as a *memento mori* for Casio—even good-looking poets must meet their end.

***Idealized portrait of Girolamo Casio with [verso] a skull*, by Giovanni Antonio Boltraffio, *c.*1500**

This grand, lofty bed was most probably made for George I by the royal upholsterer Thomas Phill, working with the joiner Richard Roberts and the lace-man William Weeks. A similar bed, made for the Prince of Wales in 1715, survives at Hampton Court. It may well have been created in 1723 for the King's new apartments on the first floor of Kensington Palace, during the redecoration by William Kent in the 1720s.

The bed first arrived at Devonshire House in June 1761, thanks to the fourth Duke's post as Lord Chamberlain, a role that allowed him to take for personal use any unwanted furniture from the royal palaces. Along with the bed, the Duke also obtained two coronation chairs, still at Chatsworth, and various furnishings, including, possibly, a length of Indian satin decorated with Indian figures and a swathe of green 'lutestring', a glossy silk textile, both of which were included on a 1764 inventory of the Wardrobe, the Aladdin's Cave storeroom of textiles and furniture at Chatsworth. The bed was said to be the one in which George II had died (which may perhaps have been why it was no longer wanted the following year), and over time it became the subject of much confusion at Chatsworth as to which bed it precisely was, given the number of richly decorated beds in the house, and the frequency of their movement. After residing in the Queen of Scots Apartment, and for a decade or so in the State Bedchamber, it was moved to Hardwick and remained there from the 1840s until the early 1900s. The bed was finally returned to the State Bedchamber at Chatsworth in time for the state visits of George V and Queen Mary in 1913, and then again in 1933.

Additional confusion was caused by the later appearance of the bed, as some of the decorative carved features had been removed, and the red damask turned to yellow—this was due to light damage, the warp disintegrating to reveal the yellow weft beneath, which had dramatically faded. It had also been reduced in height—a lowering of status remedied through a recent restoration of the bed during which 46 centimetres were added by inserting metal struts into the bedposts. A new headboard cover was woven to match the original fabric, and the whole bed covered with transparent crimson netting, so that its appearance nowadays, standing in the glowing penumbra of the State Bedchamber, is very close to what it was originally, revealed by painstaking research in the Lord Chamberlain's records and in the National Archives at Kew.

 ***State bed, probably made for George I,* 1720s**

State bed, probably made for George I, 1720s (see page 247)

The Three Arch Bridge was designed by James Paine to replace an earlier four-arched footbridge further downstream. He positioned it carefully at a forty-five-degree angle to allow the best view of Chatsworth on approach. When the hills were sodden with rain, the Derwent, Paine wrote, was 'subject to rapid floods, which… frequently rise in a few hours to a great height, and the violence of these torrents renders it extremely dangerous'.[17] From the house, the bridge is something to admire, with its glowing sandstone and two sculptures by Caius Gabriel Cibber mounted on the south-facing cutwaters.

***Three Arch Bridge*, by James Paine, *c*.1759–61**

Matthew Berge took over the business of his former employer, the famed scientific instrument-maker Jesse Ramsden, on his death in 1800, and continued to trade from the Ramsden workshop in Piccadilly, signing his instruments, including this brass tripod-mounted telescope, 'Berge London late Ramsden'. It was owned by Henry Cavendish, who may have used it at the house he occupied at Clapham Common, a well-known site for astronomical observations, for the last twenty-five years of his life. He also used telescopes as measuring devices in his experiment to calculate the density of the Earth. Ramsden's obsession with improving the accuracy of his instruments, which often led to long delays in their delivery, would have appealed to Cavendish's own belief in the importance of ever more precise measurement.

***Telescope on stand*, by Matthew Berge, *c.*1800**

A Huguenot publisher who had fled to the Netherlands from France to escape persecution following the revocation of the Edict of Nantes, Louis Renard is best known for his illustrated book showing fish and crustaceans found around the 'Islands of the Moluccas and on the Coasts of Southern Lands'. It contains copper engravings recording some 459 brightly coloured specimens—415 fish, forty-one crustaceans, two stick-insects and a mermaid, for the most part (and with the exception of the mermaid) tropical species from the East Indies.

***Poissons, écrevisses et crabes, de diverses couleurs et figures extraordinaires*, by Louis Renard, 1754**

This elaborate silver dial—essentially a portable sundial, which can be folded flat when not in use—was made in London by the mathematical instrument-maker Richard Glynne for William Cavendish, second Duke of Devonshire. It was probably used more thoroughly by his second son, Lord Charles, and his grandson, the experimental scientist Henry Cavendish.

***Universal equinoctial dial*, by Richard Glynne, *c.*1720s**

This dial rests on an engraved brass base, and can be adjusted so that the sun's rays strike the dial through a pinhole in the arch above the smaller dial. It was made by Thomas Wright, the royal scientific instrument-maker, for Henry Grey, the Duke of Kent, but was used by another Thomas Wright, an astronomer who frequented the Grey family home of Wrest Park, and who was the first to describe the shape of the Milky Way and to speculate that distant nebulae of stars were, in fact, other galaxies. It came into The Devonshire Collections through Grey's son-in-law, Lord Charles Cavendish, whose grandson gave it to the seventh Duke of Devonshire.

***Universal equinoctial sundial*, by Thomas Wright, *c.*1735**

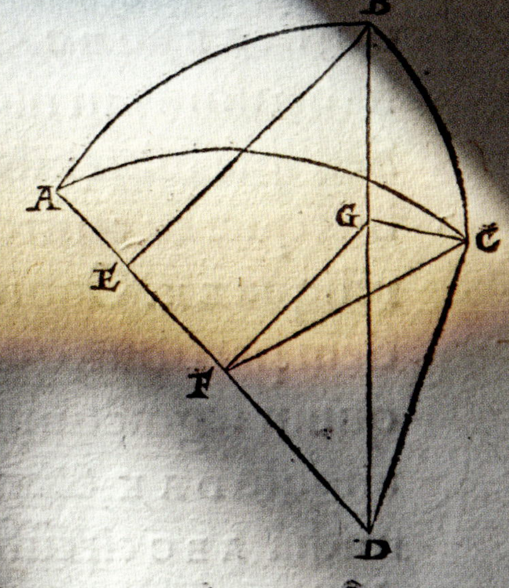

The Polish astronomer Copernicus's *De revolutionibus orbium coelestium* (*On the Revolutions of the Celestial Spheres*) made the proposal that the Earth and the other planets revolve around the Sun, refuting the geocentric idea that had held sway since the time of Ptolemy in the second century AD: that the earth was the centre of the universe—'In the middle of all dwells the Sun,' Copernicus wrote. 'Who indeed in this most beautiful temple would place the torch in any other or better place than one whence it can illuminate the whole at the same time?'[18]

De revolutionibus orbium coelestium, **by Nicolaus Copernicus, 1543**

A pantograph is a simple device for enlarging or reducing drawings to a desired scale (from the Greek *panta*, 'all' or 'every', and *graph*, 'write'). This device, which was made by Jonathan Sisson or his son Jeremiah Sisson, was owned by Henry Cavendish and stored in a box that still bears a label written in his hand. It would have originally been used to copy and rescale scientific diagrams—a process as simple and direct, perhaps, as Michael Craig-Martin's drawing of a box of French fries here being scaled up, or 'going large'.

***Henry Cavendish's pantograph*, eighteenth century**

This mahogany desk was customized to house Henry Cavendish's mathematical instruments—scales, rulers and gauges, an ivory set square and regular solids made of boxwood—by various makers including Jesse Ramsden, Jonathan Sisson, Jeremiah Sisson, John Morgan and William Fraser. They were used by Cavendish to make drawings for his publications, and bear witness to his obsession with precision and neatness.

 ***Henry Cavendish's mathematical instruments*, eighteenth century**

This portrait of an old man by Rembrandt is most likely a 'tronie', or character study, rather than the portrait of an individual. Wearing a dull purple cap and a fur robe with golden clasps that seems like an actor's costume, he looks down, thoughtfully, although with no trace of melancholy. For the great German art historian Gustav Waagen, visiting Chatsworth in the 1830s, the picture was rather 'glowing and very animated'. More recently, it stood on an easel in the Green Drawing Room, where it was appreciated by the eleventh Duke on his way to the Private Dining Room as one of his favourite paintings, and a fellow 'oldie'.

***Portrait of an old man*, by Rembrandt, 1651**

SCENE VI

POWER IN ARCADIA

n a tricorn hat and red coat, an artist is making his way up a muddy slope. Under his arm is tucked a sketchbook; in his hand he grips a wooden box with his watercolours and odd stubs of chalk and black lead. Reaching a wooded crest, he turns to gaze out over the landscape, a wide river valley set against the craggy peaks of the surrounding hills. The patchwork of fields, bordered by hedges and lines of trees, reaches far into the distance, taking in the villages of Edensor and Baslow, with their tall church spires, joined by country lanes winding around the hilly terrain. It is a fine view, and yet his real subject is beneath him, at the foot of the steep slope: an imposing square stone building gleaming in the morning sunshine. The view is perfect, the day is clear. JAN SIBERECHTS sets to work. The year is 1699.

The Flemish painter Jan Siberechts made his name in Antwerp before moving to England in 1672, where he lived for the rest of his life. He quickly took to the English landscape and was soon painting scenery with a Flemish painter's eye for detail and atmosphere. For his aristocratic clients Siberechts created a new sort of painting: grand canvases of stately homes seen from an elevated angle, showing the surrounding estate. These were portraits of country houses but also, in a sense, portraits of the owners themselves—their wealth, taste and social ambitions.

Siberechts arrived in Derbyshire in the final years of his life, having been commissioned by William Cavendish, the first Duke of Devonshire, to record Chatsworth in paint. He took his view from behind the house, looking down

View near Chatsworth, Derbyshire, with an Artist sketching in the foreground, by Jan Siberechts, 1694

from the slopes leading up to the moors. The large canvas he completed shows a moment of arrival—not just for the gilded carriage carrying two mysterious travellers in the foreground but also for the palatial house and magnificent gardens themselves. Trees newly planted in serried ranks echo the four-square architecture, while a wooded avenue gives a view towards the neighbouring village of Edensor, all comfortably within the Duke's domain. Fountains play in the parterres, around which pose stone and metal statues of figures from Antiquity, as yet undarkened by the Derbyshire weather. In the kitchen gardens vegetables grow, and, in aviaries in the brickwork outhouses, exotic birds are settling into their new quarters.

The first Duke's Chatsworth was a house for a new political era in England, following the 'Glorious Revolution' of 1688. William Cavendish had been one of the 'Immortal Seven' who had invited the Protestant William of Orange and Mary (the daughter of the reigning Catholic King, James II) to land in England and challenge for the crown. The 'glory' of the revolution was that it was for the most part bloodless. William was rewarded with a dukedom a few years later—and so the fourth Earl became the first Duke of Devonshire.

He had started work on his new house in 1686. At first it was a matter of rebuilding the south front of the existing Elizabethan house, to give a better view on approach. Yet one façade led to another, and soon the entire house had been transfigured, and with it the grounds. The shape of the old house was preserved, including the central courtyard and position of the Painted Hall, but otherwise the remains were scant, amounting to a few internal walls, and some parts of the Elizabethan cellar.

Busy in the new building, designed by William Talman (south and east fronts) and Thomas Archer (north front, and possibly also the west, although

A view of Chatsworth from the East,
by Jan Siberechts, *c.*1703

that may have been designed by the Duke himself), scores of craftsmen, masons, carpenters, sculptors, carvers and metal-workers shouted instructions to their assistants in English and French. A quieter atmosphere pervaded as the decorative painters set to work, and soon mythological figures, gods and angels appeared across the ceilings and walls of twelve of the largest rooms. These painters were the celebrities of their day. Their exuberant, colourful painting style, later known as 'Baroque', was well known in continental Europe, but in Britain it remained exotic, familiar only to those who had visited the painted palaces and churches of Italy during their Grand Tour, that voyage of instruction and pleasure that was the keystone of any wealthy gentleman's education.

The best-known painter to arrive at Chatsworth, the Italian Antonio Verrio, had just finished transforming the ceilings and walls in some twenty rooms at Windsor Castle, and also at Hampton Court. He had made his name by bringing an illusionistic style of wall and ceiling painting to England, and seemed able with his paintbrush to open out ceilings on to a blue sky filled with hovering and flying figures. In the Heaven Room at Burghley House in Lincolnshire, painted by Verrio for the Earl of Exeter around 1690, gods and goddesses appeared to tumble precipitously into the room itself. The following year, at Chatsworth, he painted the ceiling of the new Great Stairs; and in the Great Chamber, on the second floor, *The Return of the Golden Age*, in which Virtue vanquishes Vice, an allegory that celebrates the accession of William and Mary, the new Protestant King and Queen. He also painted, in oil on wooden panel, *The Incredulity of Saint Thomas*, to serve as an altarpiece for the Duke's magnificent new Chapel.[1]

Most of the ceilings, however, were painted by the French artist Louis Laguerre and his assistant, Ricard (whose first name is not known, only that it began with an 'F', as accounts books show).[2] Laguerre had trained in Paris but learnt the tricks of his trade assisting Verrio at Windsor Castle.

Apotheosis of Caesar, from the Painted Hall,
by Louis Laguerre, *c.*1692–4

At Chatsworth, Laguerre's technical artistry surpassed that of his master. His figures are more believable, his compositions more full of life.

In Laguerre's Painted Hall, a vast crowd scene spans the long ceiling. At one end, Julius Caesar's murder is being staged. In the centre, he ascends to heaven: gods and goddesses surround the Roman Emperor as his soul, gathered up by the goddess Venus, transmutes into a blazing comet. Caesar's apotheosis, portrayed here with all the military glories of Antiquity, would have provided the house's owner with a reflected glory of his own.

Above the Painted Hall, in the Long Gallery (now the Library), another set of paintings told a different, and altogether more Arcadian, story. The six panels, painted by the French artist Louis Chéron (who had also worked at Burghley House), illustrate the famous play *Il Pastor Fido* (*The Faithful Shepherd*) by Giovanni Battista Guarini. They celebrate aristocratic marriage and the convergence of dynasties in the realm of Arcadia—what more fitting subject for Chatsworth could have been found? The play even provides, inadvertently, a reference to William of Orange, who in Protestant propaganda was portrayed as Hercules (an ancestor of Silvio in Guarini's play), effortlessly vanquishing his foes.

The last great painter to work on the first Duke's Chatsworth, James Thornhill, arrived in May 1707, just as the works on the house were nearing completion, and only a few months before the death of the Duke. He spent almost a year painting two great works at Chatsworth, rivalling those of Laguerre and Ricard made fifteen years earlier. They launched his career as a decorative painter, which peaked with his great Baroque *trompe-l'œil* ceiling for the Royal Hospital's Painted Hall at Greenwich and his knighthood—the first for a British artist—in 1720.

His painting for the ceiling of the West Stairs at Chatsworth tells a story of disaster: that of Phaeton, the son of the sun god Phoebus, who recklessly drove his father's chariot, drawn by fire-breathing horses, lost control and

Fall of Phaeton, from the West Stairs,
by James Thornhill, 1707–8

headed perilously close to the Earth, drying the oceans and scorching the land. He was finally downed by a thunderbolt from Jove, the king of the gods, wearing a golden crown and riding a dark eagle, angels diving out of the way as Phaeton crashes into a stone balustrade.

In the centre of the West Front, in the room known as the Sabine Room, a different drama unfolds. Walls, ceiling, doors—every surface is covered with Thornhill's figures, which seem to bear down on the room itself, enacting the story of the abduction of the Sabine women. The setting is the Roman Forum, where, because of a shortage, men from the tribe of Romulus are capturing women from the neighbouring Sabine tribe, taking them for their wives so that they might establish their own dynasty. Despite the violence of the subject, Thornhill was careful to emphasize the theme of reconciliation and stability, making the figure of Concord prominent over the fireplace at the centre of the room. Hersilia, who, according to the Roman writer Plutarch, became the wife of Romulus, and to whom it fell to reconcile the Romans and the Sabines, is shown in a white robe after her death, mounting to Olympus to be reunited with her husband. The allusion to the 'Glorious Revolution', and to the role of Queen Mary in promoting political stability in Great Britain, is clear. King William also makes an appearance, in the guise of a statue of Hercules; the clue is given by the oranges in a painted stone relief hovering behind his head.

Many of the craftsmen employed by the Duke were Protestant émigrés who would have been in sympathy with his contemporary vision. And yet, beyond political allegiances, it was above all sheer talent that he sought, regardless of origin or reputation. One of the most gifted artists to work on the Duke's new house was a local carver whose skill was such that his carvings in the State Rooms, Chapel and elsewhere were for centuries mistaken for those of a more famous decorative artist, Grinling Gibbons, and his name, Samuel Watson, forgotten.[3] Watson was one of the few craftsmen not

Portrait of William Cavendish, later second Duke of Devonshire, by John Riley, *c.*1690

dismissed by the Duke, who was known for his habit of sacking even the most competent of artists—usually on the grounds that they were too expensive, as they charged London rather than Derbyshire rates. Watson's skill was simply too great. He worked on the whole sculptural fabric of the house—making decorative cornices and panelled surrounds, Corinthian-column capitals, lions' heads, folded serpents, great rearing heraldic stags on a pediment on the West Front, and the gritstone urns emitting golden flames running atop the building, as well as innumerable putti, shells, scrolls and festoons—over two decades, until he retired in 1711. It was truly his life's work.

Visitors lavished praise on the first Duke's house in the years after its completion in 1707—sadly, also the year in which he died. The antiquarian William Stukeley, who went to the house in the 1720s, was impressed by the quality of the stone and by the 'vast quantities of Derbyshire marble, of all colours, and beautiful'. He was particularly taken by the Chapel—'a most ravishing place', with its paintings by Laguerre and marble figures by the Danish sculptor Caius Gabriel Cibber, one of the few parts of the first Duke's house to remain unchanged to this day.[4]

Few patrons of art were as enlightened as the first Duke, whose palatial house would not have looked out of place anywhere in Europe. It was a testament to the Duke's taste as well as to his politics, through imagery that was at once subtle, puzzling and dramatic. It was also a monument to Great Britain as a whole for the era following the 'Glorious Revolution'. The new Chatsworth redefined what a great country house could be: an expression of local craftsmanship and materials, while also embodying an international style of art and architecture that embraced the new political ideas of parliamentarianism, self-determination and liberty.

View over the River Ij from the Diemerdijck,
by Rembrandt, *c.*1650

The first Duke's eldest surviving son, also William Cavendish, appears aged eighteen in a portrait by the English Court painter John Riley. Wearing a fashionable wig, silk cravat and a red robe trimmed with blue, he looks out at the viewer with all the confidence of youth. It is the 1690s, William and Mary are on the throne, and his position in the world is secure—he will soon become the Marquess of Hartington, after King William has rewarded his father with the dukedom. The son was to benefit from some of the rewards of his father's political achievements, and from the prestige of the grand house that he had so tirelessly worked to build.

The second Duke became one of the foremost collectors of his day, and had all that was needed for such success: a good eye, money—and a great deal of luck. In 1720, it is said, he bought a set of humdrum prints, only to find behind them in the frames drawings by Raphael, the Mannerists Polidoro, Parmigianino and Giulio Romano, and other highly important Italian artists.[5] One of his last, and most spectacular, purchases was made in 1723, from the sale in Rotterdam of the collection of Nicolaes Anthoni Flinck, the son of Govaert Flinck, Rembrandt's greatest pupil. The Duke secured drawings by Leonardo da Vinci, Rembrandt, Rubens, Raphael, Mantegna, Barocci and Annibale Carracci—225 drawings in all, by some of the greatest artists ever to have lived.[6]

The point of such collecting was not a mere demonstration of wealth, but also a form of education. The Library at Devonshire House in London, where the majority of the works were kept, was like a small museum of Classical scholarship, which enthusiasts could visit to discuss the Duke's drawings, as well as prints, coins and engraved gems, using the images to bring to mind mythology and Roman history, and to compare the styles of artists. The renowned collector Pierre-Jean Mariette wrote of the satisfaction of knowing that somebody so rich could also have such expertise, and take pleasure in showing his drawings to others.[7]

The Arcadian Shepherds,
by Nicolas Poussin, *c.*1628–9

The second Duke's collection of engraved gems was one of the finest in England. These tiny objects, with minute images of Greek and Roman heroes and gods, engraved in truly incredible detail, often carried signatures so small they could be viewed only with a magnifying glass. Gems, or even fragments of these tiny artefacts, were considered to be of enormous value—the Duke paid over a thousand guineas for a fragmentary intaglio of sard, showing a cow lying down and bearing the signature of Apollonides, perhaps the most celebrated gem-engraver of Antiquity.[8]

Among the paintings acquired by the second Duke, one in particular was to become a keystone of The Devonshire Collections: an image in oil of three shepherds attempting to decipher the writing on a large tomb, with a river god luxuriating in the foreground. It was painted in Rome around 1628–9 by the French artist Nicolas Poussin, and was to become one of his most famous works, with its unforgettable inscription: *Et in Arcadia ego.*

Arcadia was, in the minds of poets at least, a utopian realm, a place of eternal innocence, a world filled with the delights of love and song, most brilliantly evoked in the fifteenth-century poet Jacopo Sannazaro's *Arcadia,* a work Poussin surely knew. And yet, as Sannazaro realized—as had the Roman poet Virgil many centuries earlier—Arcadia was also an unattainable ideal. In the real world happiness is always temporary, always tinged by melancholy —thus Poussin's inscription *Et in Arcadia ego*, 'Even in Arcadia, I am', the 'I' being Death itself, signalled by the skull resting on top of the tomb. The shepherds might be ignoring the austere message, but for Poussin the *memento mori* theme was the key to the painting's meaning. It was this idyllic, harmonious, and yet elegiac, image of Arcadia that was to cast both glow and shadow over the collections of Chatsworth for centuries to come.

 Statue of Justice, by Caius Gabriel Cibber, *c.*1688–91 (see page 274)

The Chapel, one of the few parts of the first Duke's house to survive virtually unchanged, was painted by Louis Laguerre and decorated with alabaster carvings by the Danish sculptor Caius Gabriel Cibber, and carvings in wood by Samuel Watson. The room may at first appear much like a Catholic chapel, and yet the subjects chosen tell otherwise. Doubt was the cornerstone of reason in the Protestant Age, and Antonio Verrio's oil painting *The Incredulity of Saint Thomas*, set into the altar, holds the commanding position in this place of worship. Cibber's prominent allegorical figure *Justice*, proudly wielding a mighty sword, standing along with a figure of *Faith* on the ornate screen behind the altar (known as a reredos), would also have appealed to the Duke's sense of his own political purpose, the justice of Parliament and self-determination.

The wall and ceiling paintings at Chatsworth are among the most complex and sophisticated of any large house in England. Louis Laguerre and his assistant, Ricard, had worked under Verrio at Windsor Castle, where the Royal Chapel—particularly Verrio's ceiling painting of *Christ in Glory*—was the model for the first Duke's Chapel. Laguerre painted a similar scene on the ceiling of the Chapel at Chatsworth, showing a white-robed Christ seeming to sit on an enormous cloud armchair, surrounded by putti, while beneath winged angels strike dramatic poses. Laguerre completed the painting in 1691, before moving on to the Painted Hall, turning from divine to worldly power, both shown by the image of a body flying up into heaven. A detailed oil study for the entire ceiling is held in the collection of the Victoria and Albert Museum.

***Christ in Glory*, by Louis Laguerre, 1689–91**

This highly unusual print by the sixteenth-century artist Federico Barocci was created using the techniques of etching, engraving and dry-point, on silk taffeta that was originally green but that has now faded to a light yellow. It was based on one of his greatest paintings, an Annunciation painted for the Duke of Urbino, now in the Vatican Museum. It is an unusual composition, with Mary standing on the left, and the Archangel kneeling and holding a stalk of white lilies on the right. A cat sleeps in the foreground, showing that this is a domestic setting, perhaps Mary's bedroom. Yet the scene is also being played out in Barocci's hometown: through the window can be seen the ducal palace of Urbino, more visible in the print than in Barocci's painting. The luminous impression of the silk underlines the magical nature of the tableau, the colour mysterious, as if the action were taking place under water.

***The Annunciation*, by Federico Barocci, *c.*1585**

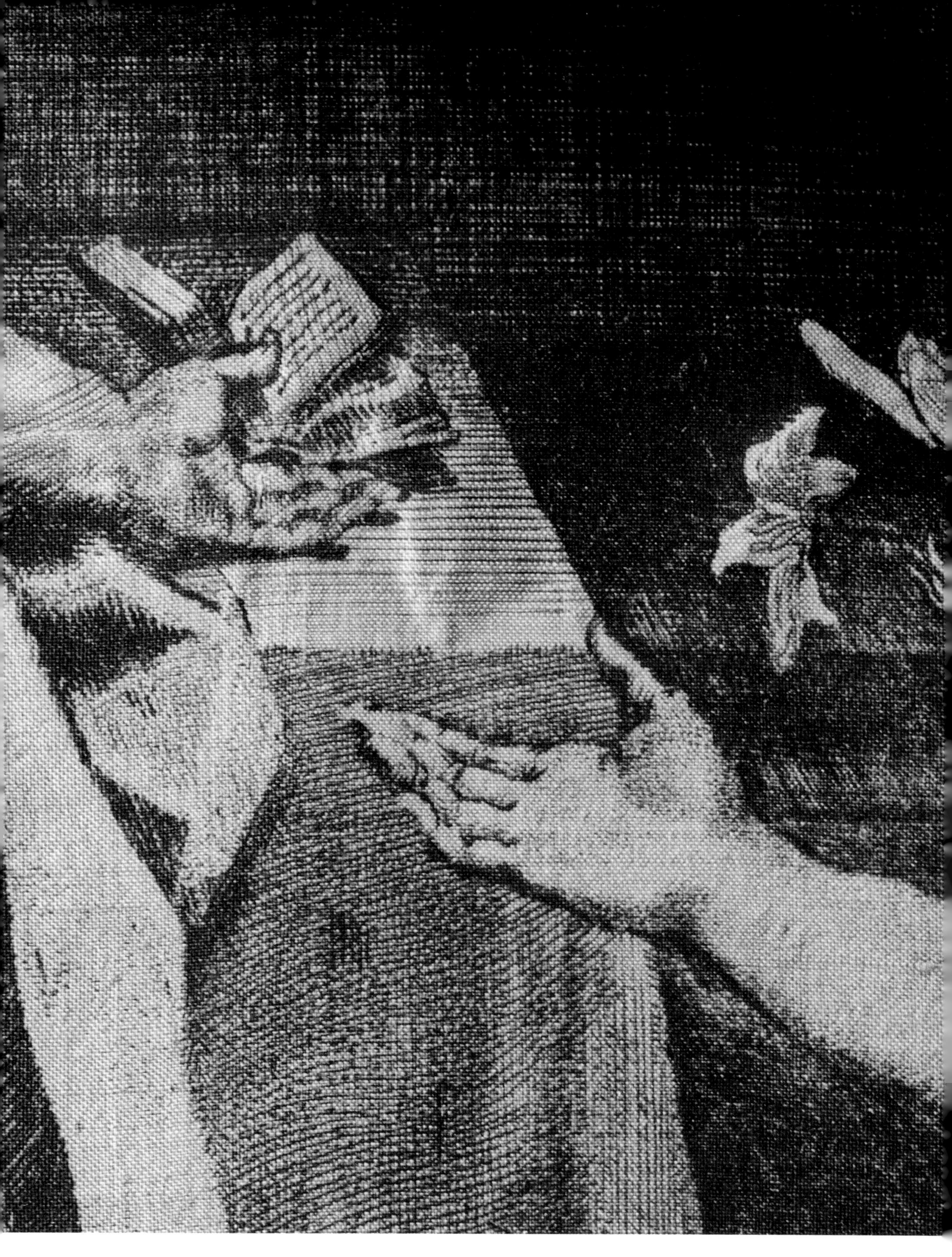

Sitting on a rearing white horse, a Roman commander directs the action with a baton—his men, soldiers from the tribe of Romulus, carry off women from the Sabine tribe to found their own dynasty. One of these women, dressed in blue and white, appears in several places around the room. She is Hersilia, who became the wife of Romulus, and to whom it fell to reconcile the Romans and the Sabines. Such a scene of violence and abduction might seem a rather strange subject for a room in a family home, but the first Duke had already commissioned a set of tapestries of the *History of the Sabines*—now at Hardwick Hall—including one showing the abduction.[9] The emphasis on the theme of reconciliation in the Sabine Room suggests, however, that it was political stability, rather than violence and abduction, that he wished to commemorate.

***Sabine Room decoration*, by James Thornhill, 1707–8**

Sabine Room decoration (detail), by James Thornhill, 1707–8 (see page 280)

From the time of his marble bust of Piero de' Medici, made in 1453—now in the Victoria and Albert Museum—the Florentine sculptor Mino da Fiesole was famed for his portraits reviving the Roman art of naturalistic carving. This sensitive drawing by Filippino Lippi, done in metal-point on blue paper, with white highlights, captures the sculptor bushy-eyebrowed, deep in thought, the furrows on his brow and cheeks like the carving on his own portrait busts. The life-like quality also brings to mind Filippino Lippi's paintings in the Brancacci Chapel in Florence, made in the 1480s, milestones in the direct observation of the human face. This drawing was identified as an image of Mino by the resemblance to the engraved portrait used to illustrate Giorgio Vasari's 'Life of Mino' in his *Lives of the Artists*, and may well have been used as the basis for the engraving.[10]

***Portrait of Mino da Fiesole*, by Filippino Lippi, late fifteenth century**

Hercules, with his lion-skin and club, stands on the landing underneath the Great Stairs, as if heroically supporting their weight. Nearby are the many-headed Hydra, the Sphinx and the Erymanthian Boar, creatures that he was obliged to defeat in his legendary labours. The wall painting is made in warm grey tones, a technique known as *grisaille*, to simulate the effect of a sculpture standing in a shallow niche carved in stone.

***Grisaille wall painting of Hercules*, by Louis Laguerre, *c.*1688–93**

Valerio Belli was a celebrated Italian goldsmith and engraver of precious stones. In fact, none of his work in gold survives—he is best known for his carvings for cast coins and medals, and his precise, dramatic carvings in rock crystal, or quartz, plaques. In Rome he became the favourite of Popes Leo X and Clement VII, and created rock-crystal scenes of the Passion to decorate an elaborate silver casket. The figures in this intaglio are smoothly carved, although their features are unrefined and the architecture of the scene is drawn in quite rudimentary perspective. Belli was a great artist, but not quite on a par with his friends in Rome, Michelangelo and Raphael.

***Adoration of the Magi*, by Valerio Belli, *c.*1530s**

Marcantonio Raimondi established a close relationship with Raphael and his workshop, after arriving in Rome around 1508. Raphael provided him with drawings to engrave, many relating to paintings or details of frescoes, which were then transformed into printed images with a technique of cross-hatching and dotted marks invented by Raimondi, and used by print-makers for centuries to come. The print here relates to Raphael's *Triumph of Galatea*, a fresco in the Villa Farnesina in Rome. Artists from Rembrandt to Delacroix used Raimondi's prints to compose figures in their paintings, treating them as a source book. Very few good impressions of Raimondi prints have survived, unlike those by Dürer or Rembrandt, making this album, compiled for the second Duke by his agent, probably the painter and connoisseur Jonathan Richardson, of extreme rarity.

287 **Galatea*, engraving after Raphael, by Marcantonio Raimondi, *c*.1515–16**

Il Pastor Fido (*The Faithful Shepherd*), by Giovanni Battista Guarini, tells a story set in Arcadia, an elaborate comic tale, by which a curse on the realm can be lifted only by the marriage of a youth and maiden of divine descent. The complicated plot ends with the marriage of the shepherdess Amarillis and the shepherd Mirtillo, both somehow descended from the gods. It was a clever choice of subject for the French émigré painter Louis Chéron when he arrived at Chatsworth in 1700 to paint decorative panels for the first Duke, and may have been suggested by the Duke himself—the play, first published in 1590, was still popular. The panels were made to be placed in between the windows in the first Duke's gallery. When the sixth Duke transformed the Long Gallery into his Library, the panels were relegated to the ceiling of the Ballroom (now Theatre), and more recently moved into storage awaiting restoration. Shown here is a detail from the scene where the nymph Corisca escapes a satyr, having tricked him into holding her hair, in fact, a wig.

***Six painted panels illustrating Il Pastor Fido* (detail), by Louis Chéron, 1700**

This red chalk drawing is a study of two figures that appear in the lower-left-hand corner of Raphael's celebrated painting *The Transfiguration*, now in the Vatican Museum. Clothed in the painting, Saint Andrew gestures out towards the viewer, as if stopping us in case we had missed the figure behind him, pointing to the action above: Christ floating in front of a bright cloud, surrounded by prophets.

***Nude studies for Saint Andrew and another figure in The Transfiguration*, by Raphael, *c.*1517**

A small party is in full swing. One young man wearing an embroidered silk outfit plays the guitar, while another throws out his arm, glass of wine in hand, and sings. A third is hunched and concentrating on playing a small wooden instrument, known as a *flauto dolce*. They are flamboyantly dressed, although seem to be in the corner of a darkened tavern—perhaps they are members of a bohemian society devoted to drink and song. Once thought to be by Caravaggio, this painting was recognized by the art historian Ben Nicolson as an early work by the French painter Valentin de Boulogne.[11] It hangs here beneath Paris Bordone's *A lady and gentleman with their daughter*, and alongside Luciano Borzone's *The blind Belisarius receiving alms.* In front, placed on a writing table, are ceramics by the contemporary Australian artist Pippin Drysdale.

***Three Musicians*, by Valentin de Boulogne, *c.*1615–16**

It is a moment of discovery. Three shepherds—two men and their female companion—have come across an ancient stone tomb. One traces with his finger the inscription *ET IN ARCADIA EGO*, 'Even in Arcadia, I am.' The others look on, unsure of its meaning. By their feet a stream babbles on, fed from an urn held by a naked river god lounging in the foreground. A skull lodged on the top of the tomb brings home the sense of the inscription—for all the happiness of youth, the freedom and abandon of wandering around in summer pastures, the inevitability of death should never be forgotten. Even in Arcadia there is death.

And yet it is hardly a morbid painting. What we see are the beautiful bodies of the three shepherds, their outstretched legs forming a pattern that, with the harmonious colours of their robes, suggests the friendship bonds of youth; the spray of silvery leaves against a glowing evening sky, even if darker clouds gather above; the muted golds, clear blues, hazy greens and greys of Poussin's palette, drawn together by a filtered sunlight. There is a feeling of gentleness and warmth, of magic even. Looking at this painting, do we really forget all pleasure and dwell instead on the inevitability of death? The enquiring shepherd points to the penultimate letter of the word 'Arcadia'—*I*. You might think the message would be lost on these happy, carefree youths—they remain oblivious to anything apart from themselves.

The *Arcadian Shepherds* at Chatsworth was originally one of a pair of paintings, the other being *Midas Washing at the Source of the Pactolus*, now hanging in the Metropolitan Museum of Art in New York.[12] Wishing to be rid of the curse of turning everything he touched into gold, Midas was obliged to wash his hands in the source of the River Pactolus—an allegory, then, of disillusionment with wealth, with the 'golden touch'. Both paintings were in the collection of Poussin's friend and patron, Cardinal Camillo Massimo, who in 1677 bequeathed them to his brother Fabio; they were separated when sold some years later. The Chatsworth painting was afterwards in the collection of Loménie de Brienne, the finance minister of King Louis XVI, and was purchased, most likely, by the second Duke of Devonshire in the early eighteenth century. Together, the two paintings tell a cautionary tale of the transience of worldly things.

Nicolas Poussin was inspired by the countryside near Rome, where he wandered and sketched, and by the poetry of Ovid and Virgil. In one of Virgil's *Eclogues*, short poems with pastoral themes, shepherds prepare a tomb for Daphnis, a Sicilian shepherd who first brought the delights of poetry and music to the task of tending the flock.[13] Poussin also took inspiration from a painting by the Italian artist Guercino, made some twenty years earlier, showing two shepherds contemplating a skull that seems to speak the inscription *Et in Arcadia ego*. It is a more morbid painting, and certainly has none of the sensual pleasure of Poussin's version. As the art historian Erwin Panofsky wrote of the Virgilian inspiration for Poussin's painting, it is an image that captures an 'ideal realm of perfect bliss', but also the twin tragedies that make this realm still human: frustrated love and death.

***The Arcadian Shepherds*, by Nicolas Poussin, *c.*1628–9**

NIC POUSSIN

The Arcadian Shepherds (detail), by Nicolas Poussin, *c.*1628–9 (see page 294)

Augustus Clifford acquired this Roman statue base while stationed as Captain of HMS *Euryalus* in Eleusis, west of Athens, in 1824. He later gave it to his half-brother, the sixth Duke of Devonshire, who placed it in the garden at Chatsworth and referred to it as a Greek altar. In time it was lost, and only rediscovered in the 1980s by the Duchess Deborah, 'smothered in roots, branches and leaves', during works to the garden. The carved Greek inscription records the honour given to Julia Domna, the wife of Septimius Severus, granting her the title 'Mother of the Camps', for her morale-boosting during one of Septimius's campaigns.

***Statue base honouring Julia Domna*, after AD 195**

The delicate, uplifting forms of blue-and-white porcelain had been popular in Europe since earlier in the 1600s, when it first arrived in the luggage of those returning on ships from work with the Dutch East India Company. Local manufacturers soon learnt to mimic the glossy surface of Chinese porcelain by dipping earthenware pots in a white tin glaze (a technique originating in Iraq around the ninth century).[14] The Dutch flower vases at Chatsworth were made in the 1690s by the leading manufacturer Adrianus Kocx at his factory De Griekschc A, in the town of Delft in the Netherlands. Their stacked, pyramidal form was the invention of the French Huguenot designer Daniël Marot, who brought the fashions of the French Court under Louis XIV to the Netherlands, when he arrived to work for the Stadtholder William III and his consort, Mary, in 1685.

That the fashion for porcelain, and its imitations, arrived in England in the years after the 'Glorious Revolution' of 1688 was largely thanks to Queen Mary, who brought not only porcelain and delftware but also Marot, her chief designer. Marot designed flower vases for the Ornamental Dairy in the grounds of Hampton Court, leading to a craze for elaborate displays of chinaware among the English gentry, eager to associate themselves with the new Protestant King and Queen. The interiors designed by Marot set the porcelain vessels as part of a wider decorative scheme, rather than simply piling them on any available surface, as had previously been the case. Mirrors were positioned so as to create reflections of the chinaware receding into infinity.

The pyramidal vases at Chatsworth may have been used to display cut flowers grown in the Duke's hot houses, although not solely tulips, as was once thought. 'Tulip-mania' had gripped the Netherlands fifty years earlier, but the craze had passed. Compared with Queen Mary's, the first Duke's collection of delftware and porcelain was modest, yet still took pride of place in his new house. He is shown here in a copy of a portrait by Godfrey Kneller, set in the wall of the Great Chamber, presiding over two of the delftware flower pyramids which he acquired. An inventory made at the end of the seventeenth century records 'old delfth' ranged in the hearths of three of the State Rooms—the Great Chamber, State Music Room and State Bedchamber. In the Long Gallery, a room designed for the display of works of art, another chimney was filled with 'delfth' alongside a 'pyramid of old delfth'.[15]

Images of the allegorical figures of Liberty, Religion and Justice, like other symbols in the first Duke's house, signalled his allegiance to the Protestant King and Queen, although it is unlikely that many would have taken the time to decipher the decorative schemes on the pots. The fresh blue-and-white glaze—and its association with Queen Mary and her arcadian Ornamental Dairy, as well as with the decorations at Hampton Court and Kensington Palace—would have been enough to show what the Duke had in mind by their display.

View into the State Closet from the State Bedchamber (see page 302)

The State Closet was originally designed in 1691 as a 'Japan Closet', and installed by Gerrit Jensen, who had been appointed as cabinet-maker to William III and Mary two years earlier. It was 'the least conventional and surely the most attractive' of all the rooms in the house, wrote Francis Thompson in 1949. The walls were lined with Coromandel lacquer, Chinese black lacquer decorative panelling shipped to Europe from the Coromandel coast of south-east India. After Jensen's Japan Closet was dismantled in 1700, to make way for building works in that corner of the house, pieces of the panelling, incised with coloured and gilt images of exotic birds, mountains and flowering trees, were used to veneer three coffers, one of which is on display here. A fireplace in the north-west corner, modelled on one found at Hampton Court, was installed at the start of the twentieth century, its limestone surround transferred from a room in the Stable Block.

Although he is better known as a portraitist, Anthony van Dyck also made landscape drawings and watercolour sketches directly from nature—around twenty-eight of them survive to this day. Some have been linked to the backgrounds of his English portraits. This is one of a number of watercolours Van Dyck made of the landscape in England, capturing the peculiarly watery quality of light. He made it during the last decade of his life, during his second residence in England.

***An English landscape of meadows and wooded hills*, by Anthony van Dyck, after 1632**

Jan Siberechts painted *A view of Chatsworth from the East* at the turn of the eighteenth century, as the first Duke's house was nearing completion. Strangely—we don't know why—it did not at first hang at Chatsworth and fell into obscurity, its surface gradually darkening with soot and grime, until nobody could recall the name of the artist, and knew the location only through a white painted inscription at the bottom of the canvas. Only in the mid-twentieth century was it rediscovered, although half a century would pass before it was acquired by the Chatsworth House Trust, in 2017, and came to Derbyshire. In the preceding years conservators had set to work and uncovered the fresh, bright colours of the original, dramatically revealing Siberechts's record of the first Duke's vision of Chatsworth as an Arcadia set in the Derbyshire hills.

***A view of Chatsworth from the East* (detail), by Jan Siberechts, *c.*1703**

Stone wall-bound icicles, known as 'frostwork', carved by a 'Mr. Taylor' and Henri Nadauld, and fourteen grotesque mask-like busts in niches, carved by Samuel Watson, decorate the wall beneath the terrace of the West Front. Watson copied most of the masks from the 1676 volume *Plusieurs sortes d'ornemens & masques*, by the French engraver Georges Charmeton, a copy of which can be found in the Library at Chatsworth.

***Walls and stairs below the West Terrace*, carved by Henri Nadauld and Samuel Watson, 1697–8**

The Neapolitan poet Jacopo Sannazaro wrote his pastoral prose-poem *Arcadia* at the end of the fifteenth century. His verses create a sense of Arcadia as an imaginary, paradisical realm, cut off from all real experience, echoing a long tradition of Greek and Roman poetry, particularly that of the Roman poet Virgil—although in the second edition of his book Sannazaro added a few allusions to contemporary events in Naples. *Arcadia* greatly influenced other poets, leading to many imitations, in which paradise was envisaged not only as a place of joy but also as one beset by feelings of melancholy. This copy, owned by the second Duke of Devonshire, is in a gilded binding commissioned in the sixteenth century by the great French book collector Jean Grolier.

***Arcadia*, by Jacopo Sannazaro, 1534**

Of the many sizeable albums of prints kept at Chatsworth, the one containing chiaroscuro prints—made with two or more tones, using the white paper to provide the highlights—is among the rarest. The Dutch artist Hendrik Goltzius was known for his dramatic chiaroscuros of gods and heroes. His image of the primordial being Demogorgon, sitting in his cave, is typical of the atmosphere of drama and magic that Goltzius summons. On the left, a snake biting its tail creates the ring of eternity; on the right, the many-breasted Diana of Ephesus sits in a transparent sphere and fires creatures and plants into the air from what looks like a bicycle pump.

 ***Demogorgon in the Cave of Eternity*, by Hendrik Goltzius, *c.*1588**

This drawing, made with brown ink and wash over a black chalk drawing, is a study for a lost painting by Leonardo, best known from a copy kept at Wilton House, Wiltshire, in which Princess Leda is shown embracing the twisting form of the swan, Jupiter in disguise. The four little gods and goddesses they have conceived happily hatch from eggs in the foliage by their feet. Copies of the lost painting show a 'profusion of flowers and grasses extraordinary even for Leonardo', wrote Kenneth Clark in his famous monograph on the artist.[16] The swirling vegetation, as well as the *contrapposto* pose of Leda and her elegant consort, was, as Clark wrote, an 'extreme example of Leonardo's twisting forms', which bring to mind Indian sculpture as well as antique sculptures of the goddess Venus.

***Study for kneeling Leda*, by Leonardo da Vinci, *c.*1505–6**

Jan van Noordt launched his career in Amsterdam at a time when the art market was booming, and made a success as a portrait painter influenced by Rembrandt and Jacob Jordaens. He was soon forgotten after his death, however, only to be rediscovered in the twentieth century and admired for his creatively loose approach to the painting of human anatomy. His dramatic style and often asymmetrical compositions are particularly well suited to informal portraits of women and children. Here a young girl emerges from swathes of red satin curtain, a hesitant smile breaking on her face. The black beret she rather awkwardly wears indicates that this is a character type, or 'tronie', painting, rather than a portrait, staged with studio props.[17]

***A young girl wearing a beret*, by Jan van Noordt, *c.*1660**

The ironwork balustrades, which seem to rush up the staircase and around the balcony of the main hall, show the distinctive work of the great French Huguenot craftsman Jean Tijou. He came to Chatsworth to work for the first Duke in the 1690s, having produced stunning ironwork at Hampton Court Palace and St Paul's Cathedral under the direction of Christopher Wren. Tijou invented a method of embossing designs in iron, hammering from the back to produce patterns and images, which might then be gilded or even coloured by paint—a technique that revolutionized ironwork design in England. The versions shown here are faithful copies made in the early twentieth century for a new flight of steps into the Painted Hall.

***Ironwork balustrades*, after Jean Tijou, early 1900s**

SCENE VII

ORIGINS OF ARCADIA

After years of designing, building, decorating and furnishing, the house is, or at least appears to be, complete. The year is 1580. A woman of wealth and standing—you can tell by the black velvet robe and the long strings of pearls she wears—walks slowly from chamber to chamber, inspecting and admiring. It is ELIZABETH HARDWICK—one of the most powerful women in England. Large rooms are lit by tapers and candles, casting a flickering light over polished oak panelling, and a soft glow over the dramatic reds, blues and greens of textile hangings. A sudden strong draught catches the corner of one large tapestry, lifting it and sending a ripple across the woven surface, so that in the semi-darkness the figures seem to come to life. It is a forest hunt, with scenes of falconry, boar and bear hunts, dogs standing ready to assist in the bloody slaughter of deer, otters and swans. Like the work of building a great house and forging a powerful dynasty from nothing, it is a thing both brutal and beautiful.

Born in about 1527, Elizabeth Hardwick built great houses and was the founder of the Cavendish dynasty and fortune. She married four times, and soon learnt that widows had greater power than wives; but it was her second marriage, to William Cavendish, that shaped the course of her life.[1] To history she is known as Bess of Hardwick, but it was a name rarely used in her lifetime, and somehow too familiar for a woman who let nobody stand in the way of her dynastic ambitions.[2] A shadowy figure, known only from a few portraits and a small cache of surviving letters, Elizabeth was the 'progenetrix', as one of her descendants termed her, of everything that came in her wake. Of the four great

Elizabeth Hardwick, Countess of Shrewsbury, attributed to Rowland Lockey, after 1590

houses she built, including Chatsworth, Old Hardwick Hall and Oldcotes (intended for her son), only New Hardwick Hall, completed in the 1590s to designs by the architect Robert Smythson, still stands.

Shortly after purchasing the Chatsworth estate in 1549, William and Elizabeth set to work demolishing the existing house so that they could begin to build their own.[3] The project was a consuming passion, such that William once wrote of his wife as 'my honest swete chatsworth'—the house personified.[4] The building begun in 1551 was tall and ranged around a fountain courtyard, with solid square corner turrets, and two slimmer towers set at angles around the entrance porch. At first it was built with two storeys; a third floor was added after Elizabeth married the Earl of Shrewsbury, her fourth (and richest) husband, in 1567. The new top floor contained a suite of State Rooms—impractically high up, but an arrangement that Elizabeth evidently liked, as she repeated it when she built New Hardwick Hall.[5]

Only one contemporary image survives of Elizabethan Chatsworth. It is a silk-thread needlework panel, showing the west front after the third floor was completed in 1577. The needlework shows casement windows and a layered façade topped by a sunburst, surrounded by entwined snakes, and decorated by terracotta roundels. These roundels were tokens of status that echoed those at Hampton Court Palace, built earlier in the century by Cardinal Wolsey, Henry VIII's fabulously wealthy adviser. At Chatsworth they showed heraldic emblems, including the earliest-known carving of the 'tangled serpent', the Cavendish family motif, and William's and Elizabeth's initials, entwined in a love-knot.

Venturing inside, visitors to Elizabeth's house found themselves in chambers and halls just as richly decorated. Polished wood, glowing in candlelight, contrasted with the stonework structure, and with more finely carved decorative reliefs, or 'overmantels', placed in some rooms above the fireplace. One room, known as the Muses' Chamber, contained an alabaster

Apollo and the Nine Muses, 1580s

carving, made in the 1580s, showing a scene of *Apollo and the Nine Muses*, a catch-all allegory of the arts. Apollo, representing civilized man at his height, sits on a cloud with his lyre, while beneath him the nine female goddesses of creative inspiration disport themselves in their various arts of poetry and music. The clever modelling of the figures reveals the hand of a talented artist—a similar carving, coloured with paint, decorated a fireplace at Hampton Court.[6]

The *Apollo* carving may well have been based on a print by the Flemish artist and print publisher Hieronymus Cock from around 1551, one of many such continental images that found their way to England.[7] The invention of the printing press and new printing techniques, notably engraving, were the means by which these ideas spread around Europe. Books and albums filled with patterns and emblems, as well as engraved prints, were plundered by artists for use in the composition of their own decorative designs.

Such carved images, biblical and Classical, drew on the literature of Antiquity, and were representative of the spirit of humanist learning which had sprung up in Italy some two hundred years earlier, and was now taking root in England. Elizabeth first encountered this intellectual life at the Court of King Edward VI (1547–53), during the first years of her marriage to William Cavendish, who had made a career in the Tudor Court, retaining his position as Treasurer from the time of Henry VIII. Elizabeth's taste was shaped by the wealthy Protestant circles in which she moved, and the fashion for printed images that were so easily translated into carved, painted, woven and stitched adornments for a new house.

Elizabeth's growing collection of decorated textiles—curtains, cushions, carpets laid on tables (they were not usually placed on the floor at this time), as well as chairs upholstered with velvet, satin, damask and other luxurious fabrics—filled the chambers of Chatsworth. The Cavendish marriage bed was an elaborate creation of black velvet decorated with pearls, gold and silver,

*Lucretia, from the Noble Women of the Ancient World hangings, c.*1570

with yellow and white damask curtains—a spectacular centrepiece for a house which had been built to celebrate a loving union.[8]

In order to sustain the level of industry she needed to furnish Chatsworth, Elizabeth kept a retinue of embroiderers, employing men to undertake the more complicated techniques of metal-thread embroidery and appliqué work. Their most ambitious project was a series of five large appliqué panels, the *Noble Women of the Ancient World*, now kept at Hardwick Hall. Each hanging tells the story of a different woman that contributes to the overarching theme of wifely patience and devotion. On one, Penelope waits steadfastly for her husband, Odysseus. Another shows Artemisia, the wife of the Persian King Maussolos, who, on her husband's death, dissolved his ashes in wine and drank them, so as to give him a living tomb. The Palmyrene Queen Zenobia, also pictured, continued her husband's military campaigns after his death, winning back eastern territories for the Roman Empire. Two panels show suicides: that of Cleopatra, who killed herself after the death of her lover Mark Antony; and Lucretia, the wife of a Roman general, who committed suicide after being raped by the son of a rival king, thus saving the honour of her husband and family (according to Roman moral standards anyway).

By portraying these virtuous women on such imposing and elaborate hangings, Elizabeth reflected her own position in the world: a loyal wife but also one who held the reins of power. In the Lucretia hanging she may well have been communicating a more subtle message: the figure of Chastity, who appears on her right in a white wimple and holding a sprig of myrtle, can be speculatively identified as a portrait of Mary Stuart, Queen of Scots, who came to play a difficult and destructive role in the lives of Elizabeth and her final husband, George Talbot, the sixth Earl of Shrewsbury.[9]

Elizabethan Chatsworth,
by Richard Wilson, *c.*1740–49

Forced to flee Scotland in 1568 by an uprising of Protestant lords, culminating in the Battle of Langside, Mary Stuart became a threat to her cousin Queen Elizabeth, on whose mercy she had thrown herself. Elizabeth saw no course but to place Mary under the charge of one of her lords, in what was effectively a house arrest. It was to Shrewsbury, Elizabeth Hardwick's fourth husband, that she eventually assigned the dubious honour of Mary's custodianship, which lasted for sixteen years, during which time Mary was held in a number of his houses in northern England.

Mary stayed briefly at Chatsworth, the most comfortable of her enforced residencies, first in May 1569, while Wingfield Manor was being cleaned—at the time the method of cleaning a house was to move all the occupants out and do it all in one go. She was ill and undoubtedly appreciated the comforts of Chatsworth, where she returned in May of the following year for a longer stay. Her first letter from 'Chateisworth' is dated to the last day of that month.[10] She wrote a number of times during the 1570s, sending her final letter from 'Chatisfort' (she was promiscuous with her spellings) in July 1581.[11]

Mary was young, attractive and seductive, able to win over Shrewsbury's servants for such purposes as sending secret letters. His wife was watchful of the younger woman, whom she called 'your charge and love' in a letter to her husband.[12] But before their relationship soured, Mary and Elizabeth were often to be found together, as Shrewsbury wrote: Mary 'daily resorts to my wife's chamber, where with Lady Levison and Mary Seton she sits working with the needle, wherein she much delights'.[13] The two women worked alongside one another on the impressive *Oxburgh Hangings* (named after the hangings' later location at Oxburgh Hall in Norfolk). The silk embroidery is mounted on green velvet, and combines images with inscriptions, mottoes and the monograms of Elizabeth, Shrewsbury and Mary—in one instance the initials of Elizabeth and Mary are entwined.[14] Surrounding the central, symbolic and heraldic panels, smaller cross-shaped panels are embroidered

Knotted serpents, detail from the Oxburgh Hangings, 1570–85

with images of plant and animal life, many taken from prints and pattern books. Kestrels, quails, leopards, scorpions, armadillos, butterflies, crocodiles, camels, snakes and dolphins join fantastical creatures—dragons, phoenixes, cockatrices, sea monsters, unicorns and a 'Rhinecerote of the Sea'—all taken from woodcut illustrations in *Historia animalium*, an important book by the Swiss scholar Conrad Gessner, scoured by Elizabeth and Mary for imagery. Other small octagonal panels show 'plant slips', cuttings of flowers and plants—a cherry branch, a miniature apple tree, mandrake roots and a lily of the valley completing this embroidered vision of the natural world.

The first era of the dynasty founded by Elizabeth was shaped by the four earls whose lives span the seventeenth century—Elizabeth's son by her second marriage, William Cavendish, and his descendants. William inherited his mother's way with money: he made sound investments in the newly formed East India Company, and also in the Virginia Company, founded to create settlements on the east coast of America. These and other ventures enabled him to purchase Chatsworth in 1609, the year after his mother's death, from his elder brother, Henry, on whom the estate had been entailed; and by 1618 he was able to pay the £10,900 required by King James I in return for an earldom. William Cavendish was now the first Earl of Devonshire, bringing the lustre of aristocratic standing to the fortune that his mother, the daughter of a Derbyshire squire, had amassed.

William understood the value of scholarship and learning, and engaged a young undergraduate as a mentor for his eldest son. The undergraduate was the philosopher Thomas Hobbes, who was to spend long years in the employ of the Cavendish family. They were, he was later to write, the 'sweetest' years of his life, when he was free to pursue his own course of studies, and also to

Portrait of Thomas Hobbes, in the manner of John Michael Wright, 1676

travel on three Grand Tours, first with the second Earl, and then with his son. On his third such tour, in 1635, Hobbes again went to Italy, accompanied by the third Earl, and this is when he is likely to have met Galileo. The English philosopher was on the brink of writing his major works, and was consumed with a host of passions, including optics, psychology, logic and physics. In 1651 he published his most famous work, *Leviathan*, describing the nature of sovereign royal power and the limited rights of subjects to oppose it, as well as the negative influence of religion on political life.

In the service of the third Earl, Hobbes spent his summers in Derbyshire, and wintered at Devonshire House in London. He was a live-in philosopher who acquired numerous scholarly volumes for the library at Hardwick, including works by Plutarch, Cicero, Montaigne and Bacon. But Hobbes could also be ambivalent about books, sensing that experimentation was superior to reading. One visitor, the renowned soldier-poet Charles de Saint-Evremond, reported finding Hobbes experimenting with guns charged with tobacco, and fulminating against books: 'My Lord Devonshire has more than ten thousand volumes in his house,' Hobbes told him. 'I entreated his Lordship to lodge me as far as possible from that pestilential corner: I have but one book, and that is Euclid, but I begin to be tired of him.' The Earl was bemused: 'There is one thing in Hobbes's conduct that I am unable to account for,' he later told the Frenchman; 'he is always railing at books, yet always adding to their number.'[15]

Chatsworth was the perfect setting in which to think and work, and for Hobbes a great source of inspiration, as he wrote in his poem '*De mirabilibus pecci*' ('On the Wonders of the Peak'), which he dedicated to the second Earl. The philosopher's final years were spent in Derbyshire; he died at Hardwick, 'for want of the fuell of life', as a contemporary wrote, in December 1679.[16]

Terracotta roundel from the Elizabethan façade of Chatsworth, 1550s

The tall, glittering windows at Hardwick Hall, and the magnificence of the Long Gallery at the top of the house, are the best remaining legacies of Elizabeth Hardwick—or Shrewsbury, as she dutifully signed herself all over the building—'ES'.

At Chatsworth, by comparison, Elizabeth exists more as an architectural ghost. By 1584 her marriage to Shrewsbury had disintegrated, a result of his claiming the rents from her estates; on one dramatic occasion Elizabeth's son William was forced to bar the doors of Chatsworth to his stepfather. Elizabeth was obliged to move to the old family manor house at Hardwick, William carrying off many of the chattels from Chatsworth in daring nocturnal raids. The transport of furnishings continued as Elizabeth, exhibiting characteristic energy and impatience, built two new, adjacent houses at Hardwick, one directly after the other. And it was as the builder of Chatsworth and Hardwick that she preferred to be remembered, 'highly distinguished by their magnificence', as was inscribed upon her tomb in the church of All Saints, Derby (now the Cathedral) after her death in 1608.

The plan of Elizabethan Chatsworth was more or less preserved in the new Chatsworth, finished by the first Duke shortly before his death in 1707. Standing nowadays in the Painted Hall, the Chapel or the State Rooms, we might imagine their previous incarnation, with handsome inlaid panelling full of symbols and riddles, adorned by rich tapestries and the gleam of silver and gold plate. When Elizabeth's house was pulled down, the terracotta roundels that decorated the façade were buried in the new foundations as rubble, and only recovered five centuries later at another moment of renovation. Who knows what else the earth might conceal? Old Chatsworth may still linger there, buried in the rich, accumulated strata of time.

An agitated, stormy landscape, and a horse with bridle but no rider or saddle, leaping from a river, pursued by a serpent whose head comically pops up from the water behind… what could it mean? Perhaps it is simply a piece of compelling visual poetry, an evocation of wildness and pursuit. Rembrandt most likely owned it, and it was presumably through the collection of his pupil Govaert Flinck and his son Nicolaes that it arrived in The Devonshire Collections, likely bought by the second Duke from the great Flinck sale in 1723.

 ***A riderless horse pursued by a serpent*, by Tiziano Vecellio (called Titian), *c.*1525**

The Painted Hall was one of the grandest rooms of the first Duke's Chatsworth, with its broad, noble proportions and paintings by Louis Laguerre of the life and death of Julius Caesar. The effect was originally enhanced by a magnificent staircase with twin curved arms made from alabaster, and a gilded wrought-iron balustrade by the great Huguenot metal-worker Jean Tijou. Later additions only increased its splendour: the black-and-white-marble floor was installed by the fifth Duke, and his son opened up the walls on the north side to give light to the Oak Stairs, adding a gallery on either side of the hall but taking the decision to replace the curving staircase with a single straight flight made of oak. The stairs were rebuilt in stone by Romaine Walker in 1911 and one gallery removed, the ironwork being copied from Tijou's work on the Great Stairs, on the upper flight.

Louis Laguerre crowded the Painted Hall with images of Julius Caesar. In the middle of it all—shown in detail here—Caesar is ascending to heaven, gods and goddesses surrounding him as his soul, gathered up by the goddess Venus, transforms into a blazing comet. Laguerre took inspiration from the Roman poet Ovid's description: 'Released from her bosom, It [Caesar's soul] flew high above the moon and its fiery tail, leaving a wide track behind, flashed forth as a star.'[17] On the side walls, Laguerre painted two scenes from Caesar's mortal life. The general is shown crossing the Rubicon river, on his march on Rome, a decisive step on the road to empire; and, in a pendant image, he is crossing the English Channel to Britain. Meanwhile, on the end wall, he is murdered by the conspirators, staggering to the ground as if he is about to fall down into the Painted Hall itself, dramatic lighting throwing Brutus's ominous shadow on to the wall behind. Above, Pluto, guardian of the underworld, keeps watch, and the three Fates spin, measure and cut the frail threads of Caesar's life.

It is a perplexing country-house murder scene. Why give prominence to such a gory narrative—is there a hidden message? Could Caesar be a stand-in for the Catholic James II, a tyrant fleeing England with the arrival of William of Orange? Or is this a warning to all those who take power by force, including William of Orange, that the Fates are already working on severing the threads of their lives? Or is it all more straightforwardly positive—is Caesar's apotheosis meant to reflect the glory of the owner of the house? Laguerre cleverly kept all these meanings open, perhaps even changing his intentions as the work progressed.

***Painted Hall, ceiling and walls*, by Louis Laguerre, *c.*1692–4**

This album of twenty-six drawings in gouache of birds, by an unknown artist, including studies of an eagle, a sparrowhawk and a duck, features a large fold-out image of an ostrich accompanied by a long inscription in Latin on the subject of the *Struthio camelus*, or Common Ostrich. The album carries the book stamp of the scientist Henry Cavendish, but may well have been acquired by the first or second Duke and passed to Cavendish by descent.

***Album containing drawings of birds*, French School, seventeenth century**

This curious structure, a high stone platform reached by a grand flight of steps, is one of the few remnants of sixteenth-century Chatsworth, although it was much restored in the early nineteenth century. It is known as Queen Mary's Bower, although there is no evidence that the Scottish Queen used it to exercise during her captivity at Chatsworth, nor even that it was built at the time. It was originally positioned in water gardens to the north-west of the house—seven large fish ponds arranged among orchards and grassy terraces that were removed during the eighteenth century by the landscape gardener Lancelot 'Capability' Brown.

This miniature of a bearded man, with luminous blue eyes and a red beard, seems to have been based on a painting by Rembrandt, perhaps one of his 'tronies', or portraits of character types.

***Portrait miniature of a gentleman*, artist unknown, early nineteenth century**

Only a fragment of this carved image of a cow lying on the ground has survived; it has been set into a gold mount that completes the cow's back. Such was the fame of the artist whose signature it bears, the Greek engraver Apollonides, that the second Duke of Devonshire paid a thousand guineas for it—a very large sum of money for such a tiny object, barely two centimetres long.

335 *Fragment of a sard intaglio*, **signed Apollonides, first century BC to first century AD**

UPHOLSTER NAILS
ACORNS FOR BLIND CORD
SHUTTER DRAWER HANDLES
SCOTCH ACTION LEFT HAND FITTING
PADLOCKS
STAFF BEAD SCREWS
DRESSING TABLE MIRROR SCREWS BRASS
WHITE BONE ACORNS
RED-BOX COPY PAPER
LOCK FURNITURE BRASS
WHOOPEE CREAMS
BUTTER & CARAMEL FLAVOURS
PEEK FREAN & Co Ltd
KEEP IN A COOL PLACE
RITZ ASSORTED
PEEK FREAN & Co Ltd
SMALL

This costume, emulating sixteenth-century French fashion, was created by the costume designer Patience Glossop Harris. It is unlike anything worn historically at Chatsworth, except of course at a fancy-dress ball. The only record of its having been used was when it was borrowed by Billy Hartington, the eldest son of the tenth Duke, as a note found with it recorded. It was stored in a small room with Hartington's clothes and uniforms, packed up after his death in Belgium in 1944.

***Embroidered ball costume*, by Patience Glossop Harris, late nineteenth century**

Embroidered ball costume shoes, by Patience Glossop Harris, late nineteenth century (see page 337)

This colossal marble left foot, carved by a Greek sculptor, was probably part of a statue made from marble and wood (one made entirely of stone would have been too unwieldy) perhaps around nine metres high.[18] A matching right foot, wearing a similar sandal following the form of the foot and featuring a diamond clasp, and broken in the same place just below the ankle, can be found in the Berlin State Museum. The feet may have been carved separately and covered by a long hanging robe. Both sandals have a small scroll-like form beneath the little toe, the purpose of which is unclear—perhaps a loop to hang up the sandals at the end of the day. It was sold to the sixth Duke of Devonshire in Rome by the sculptor Carlo Finelli, who had obtained it from the palace of the Quirigi family in Lucca.

***Foot wearing a sandal*, Greek, 150–50 BC**

The philosopher and political theorist Thomas Hobbes had a long association with the Cavendish family throughout the seventeenth century, as tutor, travel guide and personal friend. He ended his days at Hardwick Hall, in 1679, where the last portrait made of him still hangs, holding a copy of his book *Leviathan*. This watercolour-on-vellum portrait is misleadingly inscribed with Hobbes's age as eighty-one, some eight years older than he was at the time. John Hoskins was one of the greatest miniature painters in England between the time of Nicholas Hilliard and Hoskins's pupil Samuel Cooper (who also made a portrait miniature of Hobbes, now lost).

***Portrait miniature of Thomas Hobbes*, by John Hoskins, *c.*1661**

 Spiral staircase, Hunting Tower, probably by Robert Smythson, *c.*1582 (see page 342)

The Hunting Tower, also known as The Stand, is perched high on the ridge behind the house. It is one of the remnants of Elizabethan Chatsworth, and was probably designed by Robert Smythson—the leading architect of the spectacular stately homes built by wealthy Elizabethans as no-expenses-spared status symbols. He began his career working at Longleat, and was then employed by Sir Francis Willoughby to build Wollaton Hall, which set the standard for country-house architecture. In the 1590s he created his masterpiece, the high-windowed Hardwick Hall, for Elizabeth Hardwick. Completed in the previous decade, the Hunting Tower appears like a miniature version of Hardwick, a square tower surrounded by four circular turrets.

***Hunting Tower*, probably by Robert Smythson, *c.*1582**

Elizabeth R

Right trusty and right welbeloved Cousin and Counseler we grete you well. Being caryed with an earnest desire sithens the first dislike fallen out betwene you and the Countesse your wife to set all matters aswell of unkindnes betwene youe as of variance betwene youe your self and her younger sonnes, by our mediation brought to sum good end and accord, both in respect of the place we hold which requireth at our handes, that we shoulde suffer in our Realm two persons of your degree and qualitie, to lyve in such a kynd of [illegible] sort, as also for the speciall care we have of your self, knowing that these variances have greatly disquieted you, whose yeres require repose, specially of the minde; We have [illegible] though hitherto no such effectes have followed of our mediation in that behalf as we looked (although we hope better hereafter) specially touching the matter of unkindnes, calling unto us both the Lord Chauncelor, for that he had direction before together with our Cousin of Leycester to deale betwene youe and the said Countesse and her sonnes touching the perfecting and putting of our former order in due execution and the Lord Tresurer and our Secretary [illegible] we appointed this last wynter to proceede in the same cause with your sonne Henry [illegible] and your servant Copley for that the former order by us intended, was not [illegible] quiet end, and upon due consideration had aswell of the matter it self resting in our own memory as of their reportes and opinions to us declared, for the full perfecting and accomplishing [illegible] former order, thought good in the presence of the said L. Chauncelor L. Tresurer and Secretary to pronounce our order betwene youe touching the pointes in variance which our pleasure is to be observed as is specified and conteyned in a scedule hereinclosed subscribed by the Chauncelor L. Tresurer and our Secretary. Geven under our Signet at our [illegible] of Grenewich the xijth day of May 1586 in the xxviijth yere of our Reign.

The dispute between Elizabeth Hardwick and her fourth and final husband George Talbot, Earl of Shrewsbury, was so acrimonious that it required the intervention of Queen Elizabeth. Talbot disputed the fact that his wife retained a life interest in the properties being passed to her sons from her earlier marriage to William Cavendish. 'Right trusty and well beloved Cousin and Counseler,' the letter begins, 'we grete you well. Being caryed with an earnest desire sithens the first dislike fallen out betwene you and the Countess your wife to set all matters as well of unkindnes betwene youe yourself and her younger sonnes, by our mediation brought to sum good end and accord.' It was not the sort of letter to be disregarded, and Talbot fell into line.

 Letter from Queen Elizabeth I, **written by a secretary and signed by the Queen, 12 May 1586**

Limewood carvings are set against gilded leather wall coverings in the State Music Room, the most richly decorated of all the State Rooms. The carvings of seashells show the influence of Grinling Gibbons, who often used the motif, and was long thought to have been active as a craftsman under the first Duke—although no evidence exists that Gibbons ever set foot in the house. Their creator Samuel Watson had worked alongside Gibbons at Burghley House, before arriving at Chatsworth to work under the older carver Thomas Young, where they were joined by two more London carvers, Joel Lobb and his assistant, William Davis.

Limewood carvings, **by Samuel Watson** ***et al.***, ***c.*****1692–4**

This needlework panel, originally a cushion cover, is one of the few surviving images of Elizabethan Chatsworth, showing its west front after the last stage of building was completed in 1577. The inner courtyard with a fountain can be seen through the central portal. On the façade are shields showing the Cavendish stags and the Hardwick arms, and above them a female statue—an allegorical figure, but bringing to mind the builder of the first Chatsworth, Elizabeth Hardwick. The sun is shining, the fountain is flowing, and the fires are lit, as black bees and giant butterflies fly hypnotically overhead: the first Chatsworth is in full swing.

Needlework picture of Chatsworth, c.1590–1600

The Great Chamber is the first of the State Rooms, and intended in essence as a waiting room—it was here that courtiers and others were to gather and wait for an audience with the monarch. The Royal Court never visited, so that the only gathering to take place in the first Duke's time was of the gods and their attendants painted on the ceiling by Antonio Verrio, the cherubs and other figures over the fireplace carved by Samuel Watson, and the Roman marble busts standing on wooden pedestals between the carved festoons on the wooden panelling. It was later renamed the 'State Dining Room', although there is no evidence of it being used as such.

***Venetian domed copper brazier*, sixteenth or seventeenth century**

Le cose volgari, published by the Venetian printer Aldus Manutius, is a collection of Petrarch's works, including a series of poems known as the *Trionfi*, or *Triumphs*. It was one of the first portable books, printed in small, octavo format in the italic font invented by Manutius to imitate handwriting. This copy, printed on vellum, is one of the many illustrated editions of Petrarch's Italian poems that appeared around 1500. The *Trionfi* are allegories of love, chastity, death, fame, time and eternity, pageants in verse that were hugely popular at the time, embellished in this edition with striking miniature paintings, using a single colour for each 'Triumph', and an illuminated frontispiece (shown opposite) with silver and gold in imitation of antique jewellery. This copy was given to Duchess Georgiana by her brother, the great book collector Lord Spencer, who had bought it in London in 1791.

***Le cose volgari*, by Francesco Petrarca, 1514**

S C
IL PEL SIA DOR
CHE BENCHE
TRIOMPHI DI MESSER
FRANCESCO PETRARCHA

The sitter for this arresting portrait bears a strong resemblance to a portrait by Velázquez, *The Lady with a Fan*, in the Wallace Collection, London. Her identity remains a mystery—she may be Velázquez's wife, Juana de Miranda, or his daughter Francisca. It has also been suggested that she is Marie de Rohan, the Duchess de Chevreuse, who had fled to Madrid in 1637 from France, after clashing with Cardinal Richelieu—Velázquez is on record as having portrayed the exiled Duchess, and this lady is dressed in the French fashion, with gloves, fan, and plunging mantilla and lace neckline.[19] After two years at the Spanish Court, Marie de Rohan continued her exile in England. Did she bring a copy of Velázquez's portrait with her, to remind the English of her status? Her pose is guarded, although her expression is open and curious, as if she wants to know who we are too.

***Portrait of a lady in a mantilla*, attributed to Diego Velázquez, 1638–48**

Through red and gold damask curtains hanging on the bed in the State Bedchamber, we catch a glimpse of a bearded man, wearing a velvet ermine-trimmed robe and kissing the toe of a child—one of the Wise Men in an *Adoration of the Magi* that was painted, most likely, in the Venetian workshop of Paolo Veronese, in the early 1570s. Veronese believed that religious images should inspire 'admiration and sympathy' in the viewer. The splendid colours and textures of his paintings, as well as the charming faces of animals, sheep, cows and donkeys, have just this effect. A larger version of the painting was part of a set of works Veronese made for one of the wealthiest families in Venice, the Cuccinas. In 1722 the second Duke of Devonshire bought the Veronese *Adoration* in London for the sum of £367.10*s*.

***The Adoration of the Magi*, by Paolo Veronese and workshop, *c*.1571**

Underneath the Great Stairs, at the end of the Painted Hall, the Grotto is one of the oddest spaces in the house. Decorated with costly marble—and with a wall-mounted fountain showing the figure of Diana, flanked by two spouting dolphins carved by Samuel Watson—it was originally a windowless enclosed space, the base of the massive buttress designed to shore up the house during the first Duke's rebuilding campaign. Over the next 150 years it was gradually transformed into a lighter, more open space, a cool spot in which to linger in the warm summer months.

***Diana bathing*, sculptor unknown, *c.*1692**

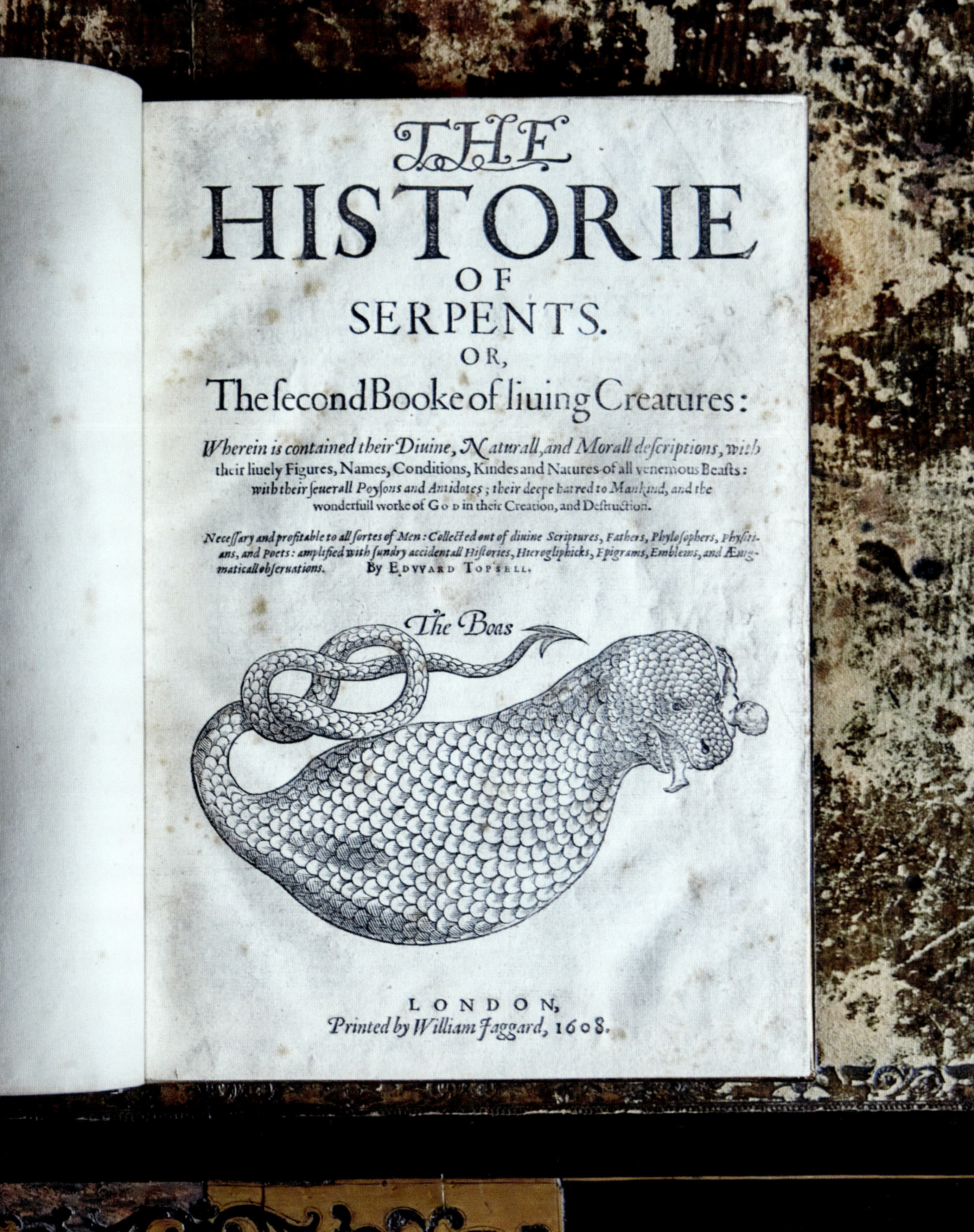

THE
HISTORIE
OF
SERPENTS.
OR,
The ſecond Booke of liuing Creatures:

Wherein is contained their Diuine, Naturall, and Morall deſcriptions, with their liuely Figures, Names, Conditions, Kindes and Natures of all venemous Beaſts: *with their ſeuerall Poyſons and Antidotes; their deepe hatred to Mankind, and the* wonderfull worke of GOD in their Creation, and Deſtruction.

Neceſſary and profitable to all ſortes of Men: Collected out of diuine Scriptures, Fathers, Phyloſophers, Physitians, and Poets: amplified with ſundry accidentall Hiſtories, Hieroglipbicks, Epigrams, Emblems, and Ænigmaticall obſeruations. By EDVVARD TOPSELL.

LONDON,
Printed by William Jaggard, 1608.

The parson–naturalist Edward Topsell wrote the first two manuals of zoology in the English language: *The Historie of Four-Footed Beastes*, in 1607, and *The Historie of Serpents*, published a year later. They were hardly models of the scientific approach we know nowadays: hedgehogs, Topsell wrote, stick grapes on their prickles to carry them home for their young, and leopards are very fond of wine. He based much of his text on Conrad Gessner's *Historia animalium*, which also mixed observation and fantasy.

***The Historie of Serpents*, by Edward Topsell, 1608**

The four Mortlake tapestries at Chatsworth, made by Flemish weavers at the Mortlake Tapestry Works beside the River Thames, are from designs, or cartoons, by Raphael (now displayed at the Victoria and Albert Museum) for ten tapestries to be hung in the Sistine Chapel of the Vatican. A number of sets were made by European weavers before seven of the cartoons—acquired by Charles I—arrived in England, inspiring the versions made at Mortlake. This set is believed to have been acquired by the third Earl of Devonshire, the first Duke's father. As the Chatsworth librarian Eugénie Sellers Strong pointed out in 1908, the tapestries cannot have originally been intended for the State Drawing Room, as their biblical theme is quite out of keeping with the ceiling painting by Laguerre of an assembly of pagan gods, with Mars and Venus making love in the cornice.

***The Sacrifice at Lystra and Christ's Charge to Peter*, Mortlake Tapestry Works, *c.*1635**

INVENTORY OF OBJECTS

4 *Serpent carving on the façade of the first Duke's house. c.*1690s.

5 *Drummer*, by Barry Flanagan. Bronze, h. 450 cm, 1996. ©The Estate of Barry Flanagan/ Bridgeman Images.

6 *A Sounding Line*, by Edmund de Waal. Sixty-six porcelain vessels with white and celadon glazes, dimensions variable, 2007. © Edmund de Waal. Courtesy the artist.

7 *Diana and Actaeon*, by Tarka Kings. Wall drawing, graphite and coloured pencil on gesso, dimensions variable, 2013. ©Tarka Kings.

9 *Devonshire Hunting Tapestries hanging in the Sculpture Gallery, c.* 1920s.

10 *Chatsworth from the South-West*, by Jonathan Warrender. Oil on canvas, 93.5 × 183 cm, 2015. ©Jonathan Warrender, all rights reserved.

16 *Head of Dionysos.* Marble, 57 × 30 × 31 cm, first century AD.

19–20 *Le Parc des Sources, Vichy*, by David Hockney. Acrylic and oil on canvas, 213.8 × 306.8 cm, 1970. © David Hockney. *Chinese Ladders*, by Felicity Aylieff. 2012. © Felicity Aylieff.

21 *Georgiana, Duchess of Devonshire, and her daughter, Lady Georgiana Cavendish*, by Joshua Reynolds. Oil on canvas, 112.5 × 142.7 cm, 1784. *Portrait of Lady Jasmine Cavendish*, by Nigel Waymouth. 1992. © Nigel Waymouth. *Portrait of Lucius Cary, second Viscount Falkland (1610–43)*, by Anthony van Dyck. Oil on canvas, 71.6 × 60.6 cm, *c.*1638–40. *Head of E.O.W. I*, by Frank Auerbach. Oil on acrylic sheet, 56 × 60 cm, 1968. © Frank Auerbach, courtesy Marlborough Fine Art, London. *E.O.W.'s head on her pillow III*, by Frank Auerbach. Oil on board, 60 × 60 cm, 1966. © Frank Auerbach, courtesy Marlborough Fine Art, London. *Portrait of Colonel Charles Cavendish (1620–43), second son of the second Earl of Devonshire*, by Anthony van Dyck. Oil on canvas, 73.4 × 60.7 cm, 1637. *Maud Cavendish I*, by Tarka Kings. Graphite and colour pencil on Arches paper, 66 × 102 cm, 2019. ©Tarka Kings.

22 *Firework VII*, by Elizabeth Fritsch. Stoneware with painted colour slips, h. 48 cm, 2005. © Elizabeth Fritsch.

23 *Firework III*, by Elizabeth Fritsch. Stoneware with painted colour slips, h. 54 cm, 2004. © Elizabeth Fritsch.

25 *Portrait of King Henry VIII*, attributed to the studio of Hans Eworth, after Hans Holbein. Oil on canvas, 217.2 × 123.2 cm, *c.*1560s–70s. *Head of E.O.W. I*, by Frank Auerbach. Oil on acrylic sheet, 56 × 60 cm, 1968. © Frank Auerbach, courtesy Marlborough Fine Art, London. *Light Bulb, from Fragments*, by Michael Craig-Martin. Six screen prints, 90 × 90 cm, 2015. © Michael Craig-Martin and Cristea Roberts Gallery, London.

26 *You treat this place like a Hotel*, by Jeremy Deller. Silkscreen on plexi, 91 × 61 cm, 1993–2018. ©Jeremy Deller.

27 *Portrait of William Cavendish, Earl of Burlington*, by Tai-Shan Schierenberg. Oil on canvas, 152.5 × 122 cm, 1999. ©Tai-Shan Schierenberg. *Chatsworth Table*, by James Rigler. ©James Rigler.

28–31 *North Sketch Sequence*, by Jacob van der Beugel. 659 handmade ceramic panels, 2014. ©Jacob van der Beugel.

32 *Walnut inlaid hall chair with Swiss musical movement.* Nineteenth century. *Enignum Locus Chatsworth Chairs I–XXIV*, by Joseph Walsh. Walnut, lamb leather with ebonized finish, 55 × 74 × 78.5 cm, 2016. ©Joseph Walsh. *Portrait of Admiral Niccolo Cappello*, by Jacopo Palma, il Giovane. Oil on canvas, 182.9 × 102.2 cm, *c.*1582.

33 *Enignum Free-Form Two Seater*, by Joseph Walsh. White ash with goat suede upholstery and white oil finish, 181 × 64.1 × 84.1 cm, 2015. ©Joseph Walsh.

34 *Déjeuner sur l'herbe*, by Allen Jones. Painted stainless steel and rusted Corten steel, h. *c.* 4 metres, 2007. ©Allen Jones.

37 *Plate from a Chinese Famille rose dinner service, painted with horses in a landscape. c.*1736–95.

38 *Watch, Light Bulb and Headphones, from Fragments*, by Michael Craig-Martin. Six screen prints, 90 × 90 cm, 2015. ©Michael Craig-Martin and Cristea Roberts Gallery, London.

40 *Portrait of a lady, possibly of Margaret of Parma, formerly called Mary, Queen of Scots*, circle of Alonso Sánchez Coello. Oil on canvas, 182.88 × 107.95 cm, *c.*1560. *Kimberley Series II*, by Pippin Drysdale. Porcelain, orange, ochre and red fired glazes, h. 13–64 cm, 2007–9. © Pippin Drysdale/Robert Frith/Acorn Photo. *Horse at Water IX*, by Nic Fiddian-Green. Bronze and wood, 56 × 16.5 cm, 2003. © Nic Fiddian-Green/Sladmore Contemporary, London. *Enignum Locus Chatsworth Chairs I–XXIV*, by Joseph Walsh. Walnut, lamb leather with ebonized finish, 55 × 74 × 78.5 cm, 2016. © Joseph Walsh. *Still life with a basket of fruit; or, 'Accoutrements of the Chase'*, by Philip Reinagle. Oil on canvas, 71.1 × 144.8 cm, *c.*1784.

43 *Palm and Window*, by Howard Hodgkin. Etching with carborundum and gouache, 168.7 × 139.9 cm, 1990–91. © The Estate of Howard Hodgkin.

44 *21.2.66*, by John Hoyland. Acrylic on canvas, 126 × 300 cm, 1966. © & all rights reserved, DACS 2021.

46 *Stellar Mirror*, by Jake Phipps. Glass, 110 × 110 × 9 cm, 2010. © Jake Phipps.

47 *Tapestry with biblical and mythological themes*, by Jacques Coenot and Jan Cobus. *c.*1690.

48 *Head of the Christ Child, from Parmigianino's Madonna della Rosa (Dresden, Gemäldegalerie)*, after Parmigianino. Oil on canvas, 32.3 × 23 cm, *c.*1530s.

49 *Sowing Colour*, by Natasha Daintry. 235 ceramic pots in 111 different glazes in seven layers and six various sizes, 2017–18. © Natasha Daintry. *Mercury by Giambologna*, bronze reproduction cast by Clemente Papi. Bronze figure, h. 183 cm, column h. 109 cm, *c.*1839.

51 *Umbrella (Purple) 2013*, by Michael Craig-Martin. Powder-coated steel, 327 × 310 × 2 cm, 2013. © Michael Craig-Martin.

52 *Warthog*, by Mark Coreth. Bronze, 96 × 43 × 32 cm, 1993. © Mark Coreth/Sladmore Contemporary, London.

59 *The Donne Triptych*, by Hans Memling. Oil on oak, 71 × 70.3 cm (central panel) 71 × 30.5 cm (side panels), 1470–78. National Gallery, London. © The National Gallery, London.

60 *Reproduction of The Chatsworth Head*. (Original bronze, h. 31.75 cm, *c.* 470–60 BC, British Museum, London.)

61 *Woman in a White Shirt (Deborah Cavendish, Duchess of Devonshire)*, by Lucian Freud. Oil on canvas, 45.7 × 40.6 cm, 1958–61. © The Lucian Freud Archive/Bridgeman Images.

62 *Guest book, 1959–83*, with fore-edge painting of Chatsworth by Kenneth Hobson.

65 *Emperor Fountain*, designed by Joseph Paxton. 1843–4.

66 *Roman marble relief fragment*, Hadrianic, *c.* AD 118–38.

67 *Sheaf of Light*, by Tim Harrisson. Marble, 160 × 40 × 40 cm, 2004. © Tim Harrisson.

68 *Sea Horse Fountain*, by Caius Gabriel Cibber. 1688–91.

70 *A man in oriental costume*, by Rembrandt. Oil on canvas, 102.8 × 72.4 cm, *c.*1639. *Natural history drawings*, 102 in total, attributed to Giovanni da Udine. Watercolour, body colour, chalk on paper, dimensions variable, seventeenth century. *Florentine cabinet with pietra dura panels.* Ebony and Macassar ebony veneer over oak, hardstone, agate, chalcedony, onyx, jasper, jade, serpentine, lapis lazuli and other siliceous stones, marble, and gilt bronze, 140.3 × 106.8 × 44.5 cm, seventeenth century.

71 *Nude on a bed*, by Walter Richard Sickert. Oil on canvas, 50.8 × 40.5 cm, *c.* 1906.

72 *Sir John Betjeman*, by Angela Conner. Bronze, h. 34.3 cm, 1973. © Angela Conner.

73 *Head of a Woman (Lady Elizabeth Cavendish)*, by Lucian Freud. Oil on copper, 195 × 145 cm, 1950. © The Lucian Freud Archive/Bridgeman Images.

74 *Woman in a White Shirt (Deborah Cavendish, Duchess of Devonshire)*, by Lucian Freud. Oil on canvas, 45.7 × 40.6 cm, 1958–61. © The Lucian Freud Archive/Bridgeman Images. *Portrait of a Man (Andrew Cavendish, eleventh Duke of Devonshire)*, by Lucian Freud. Oil on canvas, 68.5 × 68.5 cm, 1971. © The Lucian Freud Archive/Bridgeman Images. *Head of a Woman (Lady Anne Tree)*, by Lucian Freud. Oil on canvas, 45 × 35 cm, 1950. © The Lucian Freud Archive/Bridgeman Images. *Portrait of a Woman (Mary Cecil, Dowager Duchess of Devonshire)*, by Lucian Freud. Oil on canvas, 68.5 × 58.4 cm, 1969. © The Lucian Freud Archive/Bridgeman Images.

75 *Preparatory study for portrait of Andrew, eleventh Duke of Devonshire*, by Stephen Conroy. Pencil, pastel and gouache on paper, 29.2 × 20.8 cm, 1992–3. © Stephen Conroy.

76 *Large Interior, W.9*, by Lucian Freud. Oil on canvas, 91.5 × 91.5 cm, 1973. © The Lucian Freud Archive/ Bridgeman Images.

80–81 *Cyclamen wall painting*, by Lucian Freud. Oil on plaster, 1959. © The Lucian Freud Archive/ Bridgeman Images.

82 *A Monograph of the Alcedinidae*, by Richard Bowdler Sharpe, with hand-coloured lithographs by J. G. Keulemans. London, published by the author, 1868–71.

83 *Collection du cent espèces ou variétées du genre Camellia*, by G. Fontaine. Brussels, A. Mertens, 1845.

84 *Griechische Vasenmalerei: Auswahl hervorragender Vasenbilder*, vol. 1, by Adolf Furtwängler and K. Reichold. Munich, Verlangsanstalt F. Bruckmann A-G, 1904. *A very large yellow footed conical bowl*, by Lucie Rie. Porcelain, diameter 24.5 cm, *c.*1978. © The Estate of Dame Lucie Rie. *A large yellow flaring bell-shaped bowl*, by Lucie Rie. Porcelain, diameter 25.3 cm, *c.*1960. © The Estate of Dame Lucie Rie. *Hampi Form 1*, by Loretta Braganza. Earthenware, 2013. © Loretta Braganza.

85 *Flora Graeca*, 10 vols. (here vol. 6), by John Sibthorp, James Edward Smith and John Lindley. London, Richard Taylor and others, 1826.

87 *New and Rare Beautiful-Leaved Plants*, by James Shirley Hibberd, with illustrations by Benjamin Fawcett. London, Bell and Daldy, 1870.

88 *Mammals of Australia*, by John Gould, with hand-coloured lithographs by Henry Constance Richter. London, published by the author, 1863.

89 *A Monograph of the Ramphastidae, or Family of Toucans*, by John Gould, with hand-coloured lithographs by John and Elizabeth Gould, Richard Owens and Edward Lear. London, published by the author, 1854.

91 *A Regency gilt-bronze-mounted Bardiglio marble inkstand with two wells and Cavendish serpent handle.* Nineteenth century.

92–93 *White tulips*, by William Nicholson. Oil on canvas, 60.1 × 54.9 cm, 1912. © Desmond Banks.

96–97 *A Sounding Line*, by Edmund de Waal. Sixty-six porcelain vessels with white and celadon glazes, dimensions variable, 2007. © Edmund de Waal. Courtesy the artist. *Giant quartz crystal from the Simplon Pass.* h. 104 cm. *Amethyst geode.* h. 140 cm. *Foot wearing a sandal*, Greek. Marble, 99 cm long, 150–50 BC. *Head of the Emperor Domitian*, Roman. Marble, h. 26 cm, AD 81–96. *Head of Antinous*, Roman, from the reign of Hadrian. Marble, h. 31.8 cm, around AD 130–138.

99 *The goddess Sekhmet enthroned.* Egyptian granite or diorite, h. 183.5 cm, eighteenth Dynasty, period of Pharaoh Amenhotep III, *c.*1390–1353 BC.

102 *Bronze and malachite clock with a figure group of Peter I coming to the aid of shipwrecked sailors*, Russian. 127 × 77 × 47 cm, *c.*1840.

103 *A ship in stormy seas*, by Ludolf Bakhuizen I. Oil on canvas, 88.6 × 129.4 cm, 1678.

108 *The Great Conservatory*, designed by Joseph Paxton. 1836–40.

109 *Mystère de la Vengeance de Nostre Seigneur Ihesu Crist*, by Eustache Marcadé, with miniatures painted by Loyset Liédet. Parchment, 37.8 × 26.5 cm, made in Bruges *c.*1468 for Philip the Good, Duke of Burgundy. © The British Library. All rights reserved, DACS 2021.

110 *A seated figure of Madame Mère (Letizia Ramolino Bonaparte)*, by Antonio Canova. White marble, 150 × 146 × 66 cm, on base h. 61 cm, 1808.

111 *Chatsworth from the South-East*, by William Cowen. Pen, ink and watercolour, 29.5 × 42.3 cm, 1828.

112 *Reclining Bacchante*, by Lorenzo Bartolini. Marble, 84 × 152 × 60 cm, early 1830s.

113 *Dom Pedro's Emerald*, 1,384 carats.

117 *Cupid removing a thorn from the foot of Venus*, by Pietro Tenerani. Marble, 100 × 141.1 × 60 cm, 1823–5.

119 *Bust of an African Woman*, by Charles-Henri Cordier. Bronze, h. 83 cm, 1851.

120 *Reclining lion, awake, after Antonio Canova*, by Francesco Benaglia. Marble, 116 × 228 × 86 cm, 1823–5. *Schwanengesang ('Swansong')*, by Ludwig Michael von Schwanthaler. Marble, h. 180 cm, 1848. *A William IV giltwood centre table in the manner of William Kent*, by W. Cribb.

Labradorite top bordered with porphyry, 97 x 181 x 120 cm, *c.*1834.

121 *Tourmaline and diamond ring*, by Andrew Grima. 1970.

122 *The sleeping Endymion*, by Antonio Canova. Marble, 94 x 184 x 82 cm, 1819–22. *The wounded Achilles*, by Filippo Albacini. Marble, 114 x 194 x 80 cm, 1825. *Wounded Cupid*, by Antonio Trentanove. Marble, h. 107 cm, 1823.

123 *Reclining lion, asleep, after Antonio Canova*, by Rinaldo Rinaldi. Marble, 116 x 226 x 61 cm, 1823–5.

126 *The sixth Duke's Thought Book*, by William Cavendish, sixth Duke of Devonshire. 1826–45.

127 *Canova's modelling tools.* 1822.

130 *Reclining Bacchante*, by Lorenzo Bartolini. Marble, 84 x 152 x 60 cm, 1824–34.

131 *Venus Victrix*, by Bertel Thorvaldsen. Marble, h. 162 cm, 1819–21. *Mrs Thomas Denman, later Lady Denman*, by Christopher Moore. Marble, h. 75 cm, 1828. *Henriette Sontag*, by Ludwig Wilhelm Wichmann. Marble, h. 65.5 cm, *c.*1826. *Laura*, by Antonio Canova. Marble, h. 55 cm, 1817. *A Bacchante*, by Thomas Sharp. Marble, h. 48 cm, 1835.

133 *Henriette Sontag*, by Ludwig Wilhelm Wichmann. Marble, h. 65.5 cm, *c.*1826.

134 *A pair of fluted wine coolers*, by Robert Garrard. Silver, h. 29.7 cm, 1819.

136 *Samson slaying the Philistine*, probably by Richard Osgood. Lead, h. 355 cm, late seventeenth century.

137 *Designs for the West Front at Chatsworth*, by Jeffry Wyatville. Watercolour drawing, 51.5 x 70 cm, 1824–5.

139 *Bright Blue Sigillata 06*, by Roland Summer. Stoneware, 28 x 20 cm, 2009. © Roland Summer.
White Terra Sigillata 02, by Roland Summer. Stoneware, 45 x 30 cm, 2009. © Roland Summer.
group 24, by Shio Kusaka. Porcelain, twenty works in variable dimensions, 2018. © Shio Kusaka.

140 *One of a pair of Siberian jasper vases*, Russian. Jasper, h. 74 cm, 1820.

141 *Damask table linen woven with the ducal crest.* Nineteenth century.

142 *A pair of pilgrim bottles*, by Anthony Nelme. Silver, 85.7 x 40.6 x 26 cm, 1715–16. *Candelabra*, by Paul Storr. Silver, dimensions variable, 1813–14.

144 *Musa acuminata*, 'Dwarf Cavendish' bananas. *Still life of flowers on stone ledge*, by a follower of Jean-Baptiste Monnoyer. Oil on canvas, 152.4 x 106.7 cm, seventeenth century. *Sulphur Springs*, by Pippin Drysdale. Eleven porcelain vessels of varying sizes in black, yellow, and orange fired glazes, 2009. © Pippin Drysdale/Robert Frith/Acorn Photo.

145 *Plantae selectae*, by Georg Dionysius Ehret and Christoph Jacob Trew. Nuremberg, 1771.

148 *An album of photographs by William Henry Fox Talbot, compiled for the sixth Duke of Devonshire*, William Henry Fox Talbot. Photographs pasted in album, 26.8 x 21.5 x 4 cm, *c.*1845.

150 *Diomedes stealing the Palladion*, signed 'Gnaios'. Banded agate gem, gold, 30 x 24 x 18 mm (ring), *c.*40–20 BC.

151–152 *West Lodge Museum*, created by the sixth Duke, by Richard Westmacott Snr and Richard Westmacott Jnr. 1830s. *Fragment of relief head of Juno Sospita*, Roman. Marble, 21 x 34 cm, first century AD. *Relief fragment from the lid of a sarcophagus, with three theatre masks and a garland*, Roman. Marble, 15 x 22 cm, *c.* mid-second century AD. *Votive relief fragment of Kybele*, Greek. Marble, 12 x 13 cm, late fourth century BC. *Relief fragment with two bathing nymphs and a satyr's head*, Hellenistic. Marble, 24.5 x 29.5 cm, *c.* 100–50 BC. *Relief fragment with figure of three-headed Cerberus*, Hellenistic. Marble, 24 x 20 cm, *c.*150–50 BC. *Right arm*, Roman. Marble, 70 cm long, *c.* first century AD. *Marble head of a man, perhaps Hercules*, Roman. Marble, h. 17 cm, *c.* second century AD.

153 *Letter from Charles Dickens to the sixth Duke of Devonshire.* 10 October 1851. The Devonshire Collections, Chatsworth, CS2/342/4.

154 *A view of Chatsworth from the foot of the Hunting Tower*, by William Cowen. Watercolour and pencil on paper, 47.6 x 35.3 cm, 1828.

156 *Canova's hand*, artist unknown. Marble, 10 x 31 cm, early nineteenth century. *Scene in the Olden Time at Bolton Abbey*, by Edwin Landseer. Oil on canvas, 154.9 x 193 cm, 1834.

160 *A Gaming Table at Devonshire House*, by Thomas Rowlandson. Pen and ink and watercolour, 30.8 x 43.5 cm, 1791. Metropolitan Museum of Art, New York.

161 *Head of a deer*, Roman. Marble, 48.5 cm long, first century AD. © Simon Upton/The Interior Archive.
162 *The Passage of the Mountain of Saint Gothard*, by Georgiana, Duchess of Devonshire. Paris, *c.*1816.
163 *A tablet composed of Derbyshire fossils in perspective cubes*, by White Watson. 17 × 27 × 1.5 cm, 1788.
164 *William Cavendish, fifth Duke of Devonshire*, by Pompeo Batoni. Oil on canvas, 134.6 × 97.8 cm, 1768.
165 *Bagnio and Grand Allées*, by Pieter Rysbrack. Oil on canvas, 92.7 × 158.8 cm, *c.*1729–30.
166 *Georgiana, Duchess of Devonshire*, by Thomas Gainsborough. Oil on canvas, 127 × 101.5 cm, 1785–7.
169 *Rinaldo and Armida*, by Rosalba Carriera. Watercolour on ivory in oval gilt-metal mount, h. 8 cm, *c.*1720. Victorian gilt bronze and specimen marble occasional table. *c.*1870.
170 *One of a pair of bow-fronted mahogany display cabinets*, by James Frost of Bakewell. *c.*1798.
173 *Portrait of Georgiana, Duchess of Devonshire*, by Joshua Reynolds. Oil on canvas, 71.8 × 58.5 cm, 1780–81.
174 *Diamond ring*, by Cartier. 1960s.
175 *Giant quartz crystal from the Simplon Pass*. h. 104 cm.
177 *A gold, enamel and gem-set (rubies, sapphire and diamonds) dragonfly brooch*, maker unknown. *c.*1900. *Flora Luxurians, or The Florist's Delight*, by James Sowerby. London, 1789.
178–179 *A Veiled Vestal*, by Raffaele Monti. Marble, 102 × 42 × 82.5 cm, *c.*1846–7.
180 *One of a pair of occhio di pavone marble vases*. 124.5 cm × 44 cm, 1819.
181 *Handbook of Chatsworth and Hardwick*, by William Cavendish, sixth Duke of Devonshire. London, privately printed by F. Shoberl, bound with watercolours by William Hunt, Lady Louisa Egerton, and other prints and drawings, 54.5 × 44.5 × 4.5 cm, 1845.
182 *A Fabergé gold and guilloché enamel snuff-box*, by Henrik Immanuel Wigström. Gold and guilloché enamel, 2.8 × 6.3 cm, 1899–1908.
184 *Opera*, by Publius Ovidius Naso (known as Ovid), edited by Bonus Accursius. Venice, Bernadinus Rizus, Novariensis, 1486–7.
185 *The Passage of the Mountain of Saint Gothard*, by Georgiana, Duchess of Devonshire. Paris, *c.*1816.
188 *Portrait of Lady Anne Somerset, later Countess of Northampton*, by Jean-Étienne Liotard. Drawing, pastel on vellum, 83.9 × 68.9 cm, *c.*1755. Shown here in the correct orientation, the mirror image digitally reversed.
192 *Letter from Georgiana, Duchess of Devonshire to Countess Spencer*, 15 August 1793. The Devonshire Collections, Chatsworth, CS5/1165.
194 *Portrait miniature of Lady Caroline Lamb*, by Emma Eleonora Kendrick. Watercolour on ivory, h. 7.7 cm, *c.* 1810.
195 *Coronet from the Devonshire Parure*, by C. F. Hancock. Gold, enamel, diamonds, jacinth, onyx, cornelians, amethyst, lapis lazuli and carved gems, 7.2 × 15.5 cm, 1856.
196 *Stomacher from the Devonshire Parure*, by C. F. Hancock. Gold, enamel, diamonds, cornelian, onyx, garnet, jacinths, lapis lazuli, plasma, sardonyx and carved gems, 30.2 × 19 cm, 1856. *George IV silver plateau*, by Paul Storr and Robert Garrard. Silver, 119.5 cm long, 1821.
198–200 *Diadem from the Devonshire Parure*, by C. F. Hancock. Gold, enamel, diamonds, sardonyx, onyx, cornelian, garnets, lapis lazuli and carved gems, 9 × 20 cm, 1856.
199 *Bandeau from the Devonshire Parure*, by C. F. Hancock. Gold, enamel, diamonds, rubies, sapphires, emerald, cornelian, plasma, jacinth and carved gems, 4.3 × 35 cm, 1856.
201 *Collar for Hector*, by Robert Garrard. Leather with silver plates, 74.9 × 10.8 × 3.8 cm, 1832.
202 *Girl's head (Study for The Strolling Players)*, by Henry Tonks. Oil on board, 35.6 × 26.7 cm, *c.*1906. (Shown here as a mirror image, laterally inverted.)
203 *Historia naturalis*, by Pliny the Elder. Venice, Nicolas Jenson, 1476.
206 *One of a pair of soup tureens and covers*, by Paul Storr. Silver, 35 × 52 × 29 cm, 1820–21.
208 *A mantel clock*, by Benjamin Vulliamy Snr. Ceramic and marble, h. 37 cm, *c.* 1787.
212 *Design for a cascade at Chatsworth*, by William Kent. Pen, ink, pencil and wash, 40.5 × 31.9 cm, *c.*1743–8.
213 *Design for the Three Arch Bridge, from Plans, Elevations and Sections, of Noblemen and Gentlemen's Houses*, by James Paine. London, 1767.
214 *Portrait of Lord Burlington and Family*, by Jean-Baptiste van Loo. Oil on canvas, 264.1 × 190.5 cm, 1739.

215 *A View of Chatsworth*, by William Marlow. *c.*1770.

216 *White Book No. 1*, by Henry Cavendish. Autograph manuscript, 139 pages, 27.7 × 21.1 × 5.2 cm, 1786–99.

217 *Istoria e dimostrazioni intorno alle macchie solari*, bound with *De maculis solaribus tres epistolae*, by Galileo Galilei. Rome, 1613.

218 *Metamorphosis insectorum Surinamensium*, by Maria Merian. Amsterdam, published by the author and Gerard Falck, 1705.

221–222 *Playing card*, inscribed on reverse by Lady Charlotte Boyle. *c.*1747. The Devonshire Collections, Chatsworth, BU/5/2/1. *Directoire guéridon*. Bronze, gilt-bronze and specimen marbles, 82 cm × 82 cm, 1795 (base), 1830 (inlaid top).

223 *The Savile cup and cover*, by Richard Blackwell II. Silver-gilt, h. 43 cm, *c.* 1650.

226 *Virtue Triumphant over Vice*, by Massimiliano Soldani Benzi. Bronze, h. 32 cm, early eighteenth century.

228 *Bust of Inigo Jones*, by John Michael Rysbrack. Marble, 68.6 × 48.6 × 25 cm, *c.*1725.

230 *Torchbearer: A Fiery Spirit*, by Inigo Jones. Pen, ink and watercolour, 27.5 × 14.8 cm, 1613.

234–235 *The Kniphausen Hawk*. Silver and silver-gilt, painted enamel, red garnets, amethysts, turquoises, emeralds, citrines, blue sapphires, three onyx cameos, h. 36.5 cm (body) 6.9 cm (detachable head), 1697.

236 *Martial trophies*, by Samuel Watson. 1690s.

237 *Designs, agreements and bills of carved work executed at Chatsworth*, by Samuel Watson and others. Volume containing 74 drawings, ink and wash, 43.3 × 26.6 cm, 1690–1712.

238 *A Natural History of Spiders, and Other Curious Insects*, by Eleazar Albin. London, 1736.

239 *Micrographia; or, Some Physiological Descriptions of Minute Bodies Made by Magnifying Glasses, with Observations and Inquiries Thereupon*, by Robert Hooke. London, 1665.

240 *Hall chair for Chiswick House*, by William Kent. Mahogany, *c.*1735. *Untitled (Barcelona) 2013*, by Michael Craig-Martin. Acrylic on aluminium, 200 × 200 cm, 2013. © Michael Craig-Martin.

241 *Kröller-Müller Chair*, by Piet Hein Eek. Reclaimed wood, 2012. © Piet Hein Eek. All rights reserved, DACS 2021.

244–245 *Idealized portrait of Girolamo Casio with [verso] a skull*, by Giovanni Antonio Boltraffio. Oil on wood panel, 42.6 × 29.9 cm, *c.*1500.

246–248 *State bed, probably made for George I.* 1720s.

252 *Telescope on stand*, by Matthew Berge. Brass, 65.5 cm long, *c.*1800.

254 *Poissons, écrevisses et crabes, de diverses couleurs et figures extraordinaires, que l'on trouve autour des Isles Moluques, et sur les côtes des Terres Australes. Histoire naturelle des plus rares curiositez de la Mer des Indes*, vol. 1, by Louis Renard. Amsterdam, 1754.

255 *Universal equinoctial dial*, by Richard Glynne. Silver, 24.8 × 18.9 × 17.5 cm, *c.* 1720s.

256 *Universal equinoctial sundial*, by Thomas Wright. Brass and silver, 14 × 25.4 × 25.4 cm, *c.*1735.

257 *De revolutionibus orbium coelestium*, by Nicolaus Copernicus. Nuremberg, 1543.

258 *Henry Cavendish's pantograph*, either by Jonathan Sisson or by his son Jeremiah Sisson. Brass, 7 × 38.1 × 10.2 cm, eighteenth century. Reproduction of *Chips*, by Michael Craig-Martin. Hand applied black crepe tape on drafting film with yellow backing sheet, 84.2 × 60 cm, 2017. © Michael Craig-Martin and Cristea Roberts Gallery, London.

259 *Henry Cavendish's mathematical instruments*, by various instrument-makers including Jesse Ramsden, Jonathan Sisson, Jeremiah Sisson, John Morgan and William Fraser. Wood, brass, ivory, 89.5 × 85 × 63.5 cm, eighteenth century.

260 *Portrait of an old man*, by Rembrandt. Oil on canvas, 78 × 66 cm, 1651.

264 *View near Chatsworth, Derbyshire, with an Artist sketching in the foreground*, by Jan Siberechts. Watercolour on paper, 21.2 × 36.4 cm, 1694. Amsterdam, Rijksprentenkabinet. © Rijksmuseum.

265 *A view of Chatsworth from the East*, by Jan Siberechts. Oil on canvas, 315 × 307 cm, *c.*1703.

266 *Apotheosis of Caesar, from the Painted Hall*, by Louis Laguerre. Oil on plaster, *c.*1692–4.

267 *Fall of Phaeton, from the West Stairs*, by James Thornhill. Oil on plaster, 1707–8. © Simon Upton/The Interior Archive.

268 *Portrait of William Cavendish, later second Duke of Devonshire*, by John Riley. Oil on canvas, 77×63 cm, *c.*1690.
269 *View over the River Ij from the Diemerdijck*, by Rembrandt. Pen and ink with wash and white body colour, 76×24.4 cm, *c.*1650.
270 *The Arcadian Shepherds*, by Nicolas Poussin. Oil on canvas, 101×82 cm, *c.* 1628–9.
273 *Statue of Justice*, by Caius Gabriel Cibber. Alabaster, *c.*1688–91.
274 *Carved altarpiece with figures of Faith and Justice*, by Caius Gabriel Cibber. Alabaster and marble, *c.* 1688–91. *The Incredulity of Saint Thomas*, by Antonio Verrio. Oil on canvas, 203.2×162.5 cm, 1692. *St Bartholomew, Exquisite Pain*, by Damien Hirst. Gilt bronze, h. 250 cm, 2008. © Damien Hirst and Science Ltd. All rights reserved, DACS 2016.
276 *Christ in Glory*, by Louis Laguerre. Oil on plaster, 1689–91.
278–279 *The Annunciation*, by Federico Barocci. Etching, engraving and drypoint printed on green silk taffeta, *c.*1585.
280–282 *Sabine Room decoration*, by James Thornhill. Oil on plaster, 1707–8. *Large volcanic bowl – black/grey & white/pink*, by Emmanuel Cooper. Stoneware, h. 13 cm, 2011. © The Emmanuel Cooper Estate. *Eleven cups on a stoneware ground*, by Julian Stair. Basalt, stoneware, porcelain, 18×87×10 cm, 2010. © Julian Stair.
284 *Portrait of Mino da Fiesole*, by Filippino Lippi. Metalpoint on bluish grey prepared paper, with white body colour, late fifteenth century.
285 *Grisaille wall painting of Hercules*, by Louis Laguerre. Oil on plaster, *c.* 1688–93. *Atalanta*, by George Hayter. Marble, h. 85 cm, 1857.
286 *Adoration of the Magi*, by Valerio Belli. Rock crystal, gilt-metal, 8.6×5.8 cm, *c.*1530s.
287 *Galatea*, engraving after Raphael, by Marcantonio Raimondi. Engraving, 40.5×28.7 cm, *c.*1515–16.
288–289 *Six painted panels illustrating Il Pastor Fido*, by Louis Chéron. Oil on wood panel, 1700.
290–291 *Nude studies for Saint Andrew and another figure in The Transfiguration*, by Raffaello Sanzio (called Raphael). Red chalk, 32.8×23.2 cm, *c.*1517.
292 *Three Musicians*, by Valentin de Boulogne. Oil on canvas, 94.2×129.1 cm, *c.*1615–16. *A lady and gentleman with their daughter*, by Paris Bordone. Oil and tempera on canvas, 119.3×149.7 cm, 1540s. *The blind Belisarius receiving alms*, by Luciano Borzone. Oil on canvas, 205.7×222 cm, *c.*1640–49. *Bronzewing Mine*, by Pippin Drysdale. Porcelain with lustre glaze, 7 pieces, h. 13–29 cm, w. 16–30 cm, 2017–18. © Pippin Drysdale/Robert Frith/Acorn Photo.
295–296 *The Arcadian Shepherds*, by Nicolas Poussin. Oil on canvas, 101×82 cm, *c.* 1628–9. *A wooded river landscape with travellers on a path, a village beyond*, by Joseph van Bredael. Oil on copper, 20.3×29.2 cm, early eighteenth century. *Interior of a country inn with peasants at a table*, attributed to David Teniers the Younger. Oil on panel, *c.* 1630s. *The Casting Out of the Swine*, by Jan Brueghel the Elder. Oil on copper panel, 1607. *Stellar console*, by Jake Phipps. © Jake Phipps.
297 *Statue base honouring Julia Domna*. Marble, h. 126.5 cm, after AD 195.
298 *Two delftware flower vases*. Tin-glazed earthenware, both 116×35.5×35.5 cm, *c.* 1690. *Portrait of William Cavendish, first Duke of Devonshire*, after Godfrey Kneller. Oil on canvas, 72.4×60.9 cm. (A copy of Kneller's portrait at Burghley House of *c.* 1680–85.)
302 *Queen Anne coffer faced with panels of seventeenth-century Chinese Coromandel lacquer and English bantam work*. 91×117×65 cm, *c.*1705.
303 *An English landscape of meadows and wooded hills, with a square tower in the distance*, by Anthony van Dyck. Pen and ink with watercolour, 22.8×33 cm, after 1632.
304 *A view of Chatsworth from the East*, by Jan Siberechts. Oil on canvas, 315×307 cm, *c.*1703.
306 *Walls and stairs below the West Terrace, frostwork and masks*, carved by Henri Nadauld and Samuel Watson. Gritstone, 1697–8.
307 *Arcadia*, by Jacopo Sannazaro. Venice, Aldus Manutius, 1534.
309 *Demogorgon in the Cave of Eternity*, by Hendrik Goltzius. Chiaroscuro woodcut, paper size 353×268 cm, *c.* 1588.
310 *Study for kneeling Leda*, by Leonardo da Vinci. Pen and ink, wash and chalk, 16×13.7 cm, *c.*1505–6.
311 *A young girl wearing a beret*, by Jan van Noordt. Oil on canvas, 55.5×41.7 cm, *c.*1660.
312 *Ironwork balustrades*, after Jean Tijou. Early 1900s.

316 *Elizabeth Hardwick, Countess of Shrewsbury*, attributed to Rowland Lockey. Oil on canvas, 102.2 x 78.1 cm, after 1590. ©The National Trust/ John Hammond.

317 *Apollo and the Nine Muses.* Alabaster relief carving, 1580s. Hardwick Hall. © Robert Thrift.

318 *Lucretia, from the Noble Women of the Ancient World hangings.* Embroidered appliqué, 278 x 339 cm, *c.* 1570. Hardwick Hall. ©The National Trust/John Hammond.

319 *Elizabethan Chatsworth*, by Richard Wilson. Oil on canvas, 100.3 x 125.7 cm, *c.*1740–49.

320 *Knotted serpents, from the Oxburgh Hangings*, by Mary Queen of Scots and Elizabeth Hardwick, Countess of Shrewsbury. Embroidered silk velvet in silks and silver-gilt thread, applied canvaswork, lined with silk, 294 x 294 cm, 1570–85. Oxburgh Hall. ©The National Trust/ John Hammond.

321 *Portrait of Thomas Hobbes*, in the manner of John Michael Wright. Oil on canvas, 84 x 112 cm, 1676. Hardwick Hall. ©The National Trust

322 *Terracotta roundel from the Elizabethan façade of Chatsworth.* Terracotta, 14.5 x 16 x 9.3 cm, 1550s.

325 *A riderless horse pursued by a serpent*, by Tiziano Vecellio (called Titian). Pen and ink, chalk, 19.9 x 29.8 cm, 1500s.

326–329 *Painted Hall, ceiling and walls*, by Louis Laguerre. Oil on plaster, *c.* 1692–4.

332 *Album containing drawings of birds*, French School. 152.5 x 96.5 cm, seventeenth century.

334 *Portrait miniature of a gentleman*, artist unknown. Watercolour on ivory, 6.6 cm, early nineteenth century.

335 *Fragment of a sard intaglio of a recumbent cow*, signed Apollonides. Fragment of a sard gem, 2.2 x 1.7 cm, first century BC to first century AD.

337–338 *Lavender and black embroidered ball costume*, by Patience Glossop Harris. Late nineteenth century.

339 *Foot wearing a sandal*, Greek. Marble, 99 cm long, 150–50 BC.

340 *Portrait miniature of Thomas Hobbes*, by John Hoskins. Watercolour on vellum, 7 x 5.7 cm, *c.*1661.

343 *Letter from Queen Elizabeth I to George Talbot, Earl of Shrewsbury*, written by a secretary and signed by the Queen. 12 May 1586. The Devonshire Collections, Chatsworth, DF38/4.

344 *Limewood carvings from the State Music Room*, by Samuel Watson, Joel Lobb and William Davis. *c.*1692–4.

345 *Needlework picture of Chatsworth.* Needlework in silk threads on linen, 58.4 x 104 cm, *c.*1590–1600.

346 *Venetian domed copper brazier.* Sixteenth or seventeenth century.

348–349 *Le cose volgari*, by Francesco Petrarca. Venice, Aldus Manutius, 1514.

350 *Portrait of a lady in a mantilla*, attributed to Diego Velázquez. Oil on canvas, dimensions, 1638–48. *Portrait of Jean d'Albon, Sieur de Saint-André*, by Corneille de Lyon. Oil on panel, 15 x 12 cm, *c.*1530–35.

352–353 *The Adoration of the Magi*, by Paolo Veronese and workshop. Oil on canvas, 138.5 x 209 cm, *c.*1571. *Venus and Adonis*, ascribed to Simon Vouet. Oil on canvas, 119.3 x 119.3 cm, seventeenth century.

354 *Diana bathing*, sculptor unknown. Roche Abbey Stone (carving) Ashford Stone (basin), central relief 161.2 x 91.7 cm, *c.*1692.

355 *The Historie of Serpents*, by Edward Topsell. London, William Jaggard, 1608.

356 *The Sacrifice at Lystra and Christ's Charge to Peter*, Mortlake Tapestry Works. 356 x 640 cm and 328 x 498 cm, *c.*1635.

ENDNOTES

SCENE I
ARCADIA NOW
PAGES 3 TO 52

1 Jacob van der Beugel, *The North Sketch Sequence: Chatsworth*, London, 2014.
2 Hannah Obee, 'The Golden Age Returns', *Apollo*, vol. 167, no. 555 (June 2008), pp. 60–66.
3 Annabel Westman, 'A Royal Bed at Chatsworth', ibid., pp. 68–73.
4 Charles Noble and Alison Yarrington, '"Like a Poet's Dreams": The Redisplay of the Sixth Duke of Devonshire's Sculpture Gallery at Chatsworth', *Apollo*, vol. 170, no. 570 (2009), pp. 46–53.
5 Adolf Furtwängler, 'Ancient Sculptures at Chatsworth House', *Journal of Hellenic Studies*, vol. 21 (1901), pp. 209–28.

SCENE II
TROUBLE IN ARCADIA
PAGES 55 TO 104

1 'The Problem of the Country House', *Burlington Magazine for Connoisseurs*, vol. 83, no. 484 (July 1943), pp. 159–60.
2 Francis Thompson to the tenth Duke, 13 February 1945, The Devonshire Collections, Chatsworth, CH 12/4/4.
3 Deborah, Duchess of Devonshire, *Chatsworth: The House* (London, 2002), p. 55.
4 David Cannadine, 'The Landowner as Millionaire: The Finances of the Dukes of Devonshire, 1800–*c.*1926', *Agricultural History Review*, vol. 25, no. 2 (1977), pp. 77–97 (83).
5 Ibid., p. 87.
6 Spencer Compton Cavendish, eighth Duke of Devonshire to Lady Louisa Egerton, 6 April 1894, The Devonshire Collections, Chatsworth, CS 8/340/2551.
7 Cannadine, p. 90.
8 Andrew Cavendish, eleventh Duke of Devonshire, *Accidents of Fortune* (London, 2004), p. 45.
9 'A National Museum? The Future of Chatsworth', *Manchester Guardian*, 19 June 1954.
10 'Hardwick and the Chatsworth Treasures', *Burlington Magazine*, vol. 99, no. 655 (October 1957), pp. 327–8; 'Negotiations on Hardwick Hall: Acceptance by Treasury Sought', *The Times*, 18 August 1956.
11 Ludwig Ross, *A Journey to Cyprus*, trans. Claude Deleval Cobham (Nicosia, 1910), p. 73.
12 Sculpture Accounts, The Devonshire Collections, Chatsworth, DF 4/1/14/1, f. 31.
13 William Feaver, *The Lives of Lucian Freud: Youth 1922–1968* (London, 2019), p. 477.
14 Ibid., p. 276.
15 Deborah Cavendish, Duchess of Devonshire to Patrick Leigh Fermor, 22 July 1958, *In Tearing Haste: Letters between Deborah Devonshire and Patrick Leigh Fermor* (London, 2008), p. 47.
16 Eugénie Sellers Strong, *Roman Sculpture from Augustus to Constantine* (London, 1907), pp. 235–6.
17 Christopher Nicholson, 'In the Slow Zone', in *Tim Harrisson: As It Was Is Now*, exhibition catalogue, Messums Wiltshire (Salisbury, 2018), pp. 2–5.
18 Feaver, *The Lives of Lucian Freud: Youth*, p. 478.
19 William Feaver, *The Lives of Lucian Freud: Fame 1968–2011* (London, 2020), p. 38.
20 Ibid., p. 27.
21 Anne Wilkins, 'The Preternatural Gardener: The Life of James Shirley Hibberd (1825–90)', *Garden History*, vol. 26, no. 2 (Winter 1998), pp. 153–75.

SCENE III
AMBITION IN ARCADIA
PAGES 107 TO 156

1 William Cavendish, sixth Duke of Devonshire, *Handbook of Chatsworth and Hardwick*, London, privately printed, 1845, p. 119.
2 Hugh Honour, 'Canova's Studio Practice. II: 1792–1822', *Burlington Magazine*, vol. 114, no. 829 (April 1972), pp. 214–29.
3 Sixth Duke's 'Thought Book', 1817, The Devonshire Collections, Chatsworth, DF 4/2/2/1, f. 10.
4 *Handbook*, p. 105.
5 Ibid.
6 Alison Yarrington, '"Under Italian Skies": The Sixth Duke of Devonshire, Canova, and the Formation of a Sculpture Gallery at Chatsworth House', *Journal of Anglo-Italian Studies*, vol. 10 (2009), pp. 41–62.

7 Charles Noble and Alison Yarrington, '"Like a Poet's Dreams": The Redisplay of the Sixth Duke of Devonshire's Sculpture Gallery at Chatsworth', *Apollo*, vol. 170, no. 570 (2009), pp. 46–53.
8 Ibid.
9 John Kenworthy-Browne, 'A Ducal Patron of Sculptors', *Apollo*, vol. 96, no. 128 (1972), pp. 322–31 (330); *Handbook*, p. 103.
10 Yarrington, pp. 41–62.
11 *Le Modèle noir: De Géricault à Matisse*, exhibition catalogue, Musée d'Orsay, Paris, 2019, p. 57. See also: Charmaine Nelson, 'Vénus Africaine: Race, Beauty and African-ness', in Jan Marsh (ed.), *Black Victorians: Black People in British Art 1800–1900* (London, 2005), pp. 46–56.
12 Hugh Honour, *The Image of the Black in Western Art. Vol. 4: From the American Revolution to World War I*, 'Part 2: Black Models and White Myths' (Cambridge, Mass., and London, 1989), p. 101.
13 *Le Modèle noir*, p. 121.
14 Honour, *The Image of the Black in Western Art*, p. 104.
15 Barbara Larson, 'The Artist as Ethnographer: Charles Cordier and Race in Mid-Nineteenth-Century France', *The Art Bulletin*, vol. 87, no. 4 (December 2005), pp. 714–22 (718).
16 Francis Haskell and Nicholas Penny, *Taste and the Antique: The Lure of Classical Sculpture 1500–1900* (New Haven, 1981), pp. 322–3.
17 George Ferris, *Great Singers: Faustina Bordoni to Henriette Sontag* (New York, 1879), p. 197.
18 *Life of Henriette Sontag, Countess di Rossi, with Interesting Sketches by Scudo, Hector Berlioz, Louis Boerne, Adolphe Adam, Marie Aycard, Julie de Margueriete, Prince Puckler-Muskau and Théophile Gautier* (New York, 1852), p. 21.
19 Wilfrid Blunt, *G. D. Ehret* (Guildford, 1953).
20 Giles Worsley, *The British Stable* (New Haven, 2004), p. 141.

SCENE IV
EXILE FROM ARCADIA
PAGES 159 TO 208

1 Iris Leveson-Gower, *The Face without a Frown* (London, 1944), p. 179.
2 Ibid., p. 182.
3 Quoted by Mick Cooper, 'The Devonshire Mineral Collection of Chatsworth House: An Eighteenth-Century Survivor and Its Restoration', *Mineralogical Record*, vol. 36, no. 3 (May–June 2005), p. 244.
4 Thompson was also known as Count Rumford, and went down in history not only as an intelligence agent but also as a founding figure in the field of thermodynamics.
5 'Catalogue of External Characters of Fossils, by White Watson F.L.S., Bakewell, Derbyshire, 1798', MS, The Devonshire Collections, Chatsworth, C 194.
6 Memo by Mr White Watson, Bakewell, The Devonshire Collections, Chatsworth, CH 37/9.
7 Cooper, pp. 239–74.
8 Nicolas Barker, 'The Collections at Chatsworth', in Nicolas Barker (ed.), *The Devonshire Inheritance: Five Centuries of Collecting at Chatsworth* (Alexandria, Virginia, 2003), pp. 22–41 (35).
9 Ibid., p. 24.
10 Allan Cunningham, 'Gainsborough', in *The Lives of the Most Eminent British Painters, Sculptors, and Architects*, vol. 1 (London, 1829), p. 335.
11 William Cavendish, sixth Duke of Devonshire, *Handbook of Chatsworth and Hardwick* (London, privately printed, 1845), p. 146.
12 Helen Clifford, 'Chinese Wallpaper: From Canton to Country House', in Margot Finn and Kate Smith (eds.), *East India Company at Home 1757–1857* (London, 2018), pp. 39–67.
13 Christopher Baker, William Hauptmann and Mary Anne Stevens (eds.), *Jean-Étienne Liotard 1702–1789*, exhibition catalogue, Royal Academy (London, 2015).
14 Diana Scarisbrick, 'The Devonshire Gems and Parure', in Barker (ed.), *The Devonshire Inheritance*, pp. 64–73.
15 C. H. Collins Baker, 'The Paintings of Professor Henry Tonks', *The Studio*, vol. 49, no. 203, (February 1910), pp. 3–10 (4, 6).

SCENE V
CURIOSITY IN ARCADIA
PAGES 211 TO 260

1 John Barnatt and Tom Williamson, *Chatsworth: A Landscape History* (Cheshire, 2005), pp. 96–7.
2 Ibid., p. 105.
3 Peter Leach, *James Paine* (London, 1988), pp. 117–21.
4 Horace Walpole to the Earl of Strafford, 4 September 1760. *The Letters of Horace Walpole, Earl of Orford*, vol. 4 (London, 1840), p. 89.

5 Horace Walpole to George Montagu, 1 September 1760. Ibid., p. 84.
6 James Lees-Milne, *Earls of Creation: Five Great Patrons of Eighteenth-Century Art* (London, 1962), p. 111.
7 Mark Girouard, 'Lismore', *Country Life*, 6 August 1964, p. 340.
8 *Pallas Unveil'd: The Life and Art of Lady Dorothy Savile, Countess of Burlington (1699–1758)*, exhibition catalogue, Orleans House Gallery (Twickenham, 1999).
9 Horace Walpole, *Anecdotes of Painting in England* (London, 1871), p. 382.
10 A. J. Berry, *Henry Cavendish: His Life and Scientific Work* (London, 1960), pp. 25–6.
11 Ibid., p. 11.
12 Christa Jungnickel and Russell McCormmach, *Cavendish: The Experimental Life* (rev. 2nd edn), Edition Open Access, 2016, p. 431.
13 Eric J. G. Smith, 'Richard Blackwell & Son', *Silver Society Journal*, no. 15 (2003), pp. 19–33.
14 Roy Strong, *Festival Designs by Inigo Jones: An Exhibition of Drawings and Scenery and Costumes for the Court Masques of James I and Charles I* (Washington, DC, 1967/8).
15 Thomas Campion, *Description, Speeches, and Songs, of the Lords Maske, presented in the Banquetting-house on the Mariage Night of the High and Mightie Count Palantine, and the Royally Descended the Ladie Elizabeth* (London, 1613).
16 Peter Osborne, 'Eleazar Albin', *Dictionary of National Biography* (23 September 2004).
17 James Paine, *Plans, Elevations and Sections of Noblemen's and Gentlemen's Houses* (London, 1767), p. ii.
18 *De revolutionibus orbium celestium*, trans. W. C. D. and M. D. Whetham, Cambridge Readings in the Literature of Science (Cambridge, 1924), p. 13.

SCENE VI
POWER IN ARCADIA
PAGES 263 TO 312

1 Cécile Brett, 'Antonio Verrio (*c.* 1636–1707): His Career and Surviving Work', *British Art Journal*, vol. 10, no. 3 (Winter/Spring, 2009/10), pp. 4–17.
2 Chatsworth Building Accounts 1687–94, The Devonshire Collections, Chatsworth, CH 37/8, f. 38.
3 Trevor Brighton, 'Samuel Watson, Not Grinling Gibbons, at Chatsworth', *Burlington Magazine*, vol. 140, no. 1,149 (December 1998), pp. 811–18.
4 William Stukeley, *Itinerarium curiosum; or, an Account of the Antiquitys and Remarkable Curiositys in Nature or Art, Observ'd in Travels thro' Great Britain* (London, 1724), pp. 55–6.
5 Michael Jaffé, *The Devonshire Collection of Northern European Drawings*, vol. 1 (Turin, 2002), p. 16.
6 Arnold Houbraken, *De groote schouburgh der Nederlantsche konstschilders en schilderessen*, vol. 2 (Amsterdam, 1718–21), p. 23.
7 Cited by Michael Jaffé, *The Devonshire Collection of Italian Drawings, Tuscan and Umbrian Schools* (London, 1994), p. 16.
8 Diana Scarisbrick, 'The Devonshire Gems and Parure', in Nicolas Barker (ed.), *The Devonshire Inheritance: Five Centuries of Collecting at Chatsworth* (Alexandria, Virginia, 2003), pp. 64–73 (70).
9 Helen Wyld, 'Seventeenth-century Tapestries at Hardwick Hall: Sources and Iconography', in David Adshead and David A. H. B. Taylor (eds.), *Hardwick Hall: A Great Old Castle of Romance* (New Haven, 2016), pp. 209–221 (217–20).
10 George R. Goldner and Carmen Bambach, *The Drawings of Filippino Lippi and His Circle* (New York, 1997), p. 136.
11 Benedict Nicolson, *The International Caravaggesque Movement: Lists of Pictures by Caravaggio and His Followers throughout Europe from 1590 to 1650* (London, 1979), p. 106. Nicolson also lists a copy of Caravaggio's *Calling of Saints Peter and Andrew*, which was sold in 1976, and a copy by Anthony van Dyck of Orazio Gentileschi's *Judith and Holofernes* as being at Chatsworth.
12 Anthony Blunt, 'Poussin's *Et in Arcadia ego*', *Art Bulletin*, vol. 20, no. 1 (March 1938), pp. 96–100.
13 Erwin Panofsky, '*Et in Arcadia ego*: Poussin and the Elegiac Tradition', *Meaning in the Visual Arts* (New York, 1955).
14 Hannah Obee, 'Baroque Exuberance: Delft Flower Vases at Chatsworth', *Apollo*, vol. 167, no. 555 (2008), pp. 90–97.
15 Ibid.
16 Kenneth Clark, *Leonardo da Vinci* (1939; London, 1993), p. 180.
17 David A. de Witt, *Jan van Noordt: Painter of History and Portraits in Amsterdam* (Montreal, 2007), pp. 161–2.

SCENE VII
ORIGINS OF ARCADIA
PAGES 315 TO 364

1 Kate Hubbard, *Devices & Desires: Bess of Hardwick and the Building of Elizabethan England* (London, 2018), p. 13.
2 Ibid., p. xxiv.
3 Francis Thompson, *A History of Chatsworth* (London, 1949), p. 21.
4 Folger Shakespeare Library, Cavendish–Talbot MSS, X.d.428 (77).
5 Mark Girouard, 'Elizabethan Chatsworth', *Country Life*, 22 November 1973, pp. 1,668–72.
6 It is now in the Victoria and Albert Museum.
7 Anthony Wells-Cole, *Art and Decoration in Elizabethan and Jacobean England: The Influence of Continental Prints, 1558–1625* (New Haven, 1997), p. 254.
8 Emma Slocombe, 'The Embroidery and Needlework of Bess of Hardwick', in David Adshead and David A. H. B. Taylor (eds.), *Hardwick Hall: A Great Old Castle of Romance* (New Haven, 2016), pp. 110–32 (112).
9 The identification is made by Anthony Wells-Cole, p. 258.
10 Agnes Strickland (ed.), *Letters of Mary, Queen of Scots*, vol. 1 (London, 1843), p. 217.
11 Alexandre Labanoff (ed.), *Recueil des lettres de Marie Stuart, reine d'Écosse*, vol. 5 (London, 1844), p. 238.
12 Hubbard, p. 138.
13 George Talbot, Earl of Shrewsbury, to William Cecil, March 1659; cited by Hubbard, p. 101.
14 Michael Bath, *Emblems for a Queen: The Needlework of Mary, Queen of Scots* (London, 2008), p. 11.
15 Steven Glover, *The Peak Guide, etc* (Derby, 1830), p. 39.
16 Cited in Noel Malcolm, 'Thomas Hobbes', *Dictionary of National Biography* (23 September 2010).
17 Ovid, *Metamorphoses*, trans. Mary M. Innes (Harmondsworth, 1955), p. 357.
18 D. Boschung, H. von Hesberg and A. Linfert, *Die antiken Skulpturen in Chatsworth: sowie in Dunham Massey und Withington Hall, Monumenta artis romanae*, vol. 26 (Mainz am Rhein, 1997), pp. 44–5, no. 42, pls. 35, 5.
19 Zahira Veliz, 'Signs of Identity in *Lady with a Fan* by Diego Velázquez: Costume and Likeness Reconsidered', *Art Bulletin*, vol. 86, no. 1 (March 2004), pp. 75–95.

SELECTED READING

William Cavendish, sixth Duke of Devonshire: *Handbook of Chatsworth and Hardwick*. 1845. Facsimile, ed. John Martin Robinson, printed for the Roxburghe Club, 2020.

Francis Thompson: *A History of Chatsworth*. London, 1949.

Brian Masters: *Georgiana, Duchess of Devonshire*. London, 1981.

James Lees-Milne: *The Bachelor Duke: A Life of William Spencer Cavendish, sixth Duke of Devonshire, 1790–1858*. London, 1990.

Michael Jaffé: *The Devonshire Collection of Italian Drawings*, 4 vols. London, 1994.

Amanda Foreman: *Georgiana, Duchess of Devonshire*. London, 1998.

Deborah Cavendish, Duchess of Devonshire: *Chatsworth: The House*. London, 2002.

Michael Jaffé, *The Devonshire Collection of Northern European Drawings*, 5 vols. London, 2002.

Nicolas Barker (ed.): *The Devonshire Inheritance: Five Centuries of Collecting at Chatsworth*. Alexandria, Virginia, 2003.

Kate Colquhoun: *A Thing in Disguise: The Visionary Life of Joseph Paxton*. London, 2003.

Andrew Cavendish, eleventh Duke of Devonshire: *Accidents of Fortune*. London, 2004.

David Adshead, David A. H. B. Taylor (eds.): *Hardwick Hall: A Great Old Castle of Romance*. New Haven, 2016.

Kate Hubbard: *Devices & Desires: Bess of Hardwick and the Building of Elizabethan England*. London, 2018.

ACKNOWLEDGEMENTS

The creation of *Chatsworth, Arcadia, Now* has been a collaboration involving a cast of hundreds.

At Chatsworth, the curatorial team—Alex Hodby (contemporary art), Sash Giles (decorative arts), Susie Stokoe (textiles), Diane Naylor (photography) and, in particular, Charles Noble (fine arts)—patiently and succinctly answered many questions about The Devonshire Collections. In the archive, James Towe and his successors Fran Baker and Aiden Haley responded to numerous queries of often excruciating detail. Ted Cadogan, Kate Brindley, Alice Martin, Denna Garrett, Luke Stones, Dorothy Rayner and Ian Groom facilitated research visits and photography. The house guides and those in the private household—Mollie Moseley, Kay Rotchford, Julia Goldsmith and Tom Biddle—fielded all manner of enquiries about the house and grounds; as did Sean Doxey, Steve Porter and Shenagh Firth. Helen Marchant oversaw the project from beginning to end, deftly guiding it through snowstorms, floods and a pandemic.

Beyond Chatsworth, the following people offered advice, encouragement and ideas: Stuart Band, Jacob van der Beugel, Glenn Brown, Sarah Cavalier, Hugo Chapman, Rob Cooper, Bart Cornelis, Michael Craig-Martin, Natasha Daintry, David Dawson, Peter Day, Jeremy Deller, Donato Esposito, Lara Feigel, Katie Graham, Antony Griffiths, Richard Higgins, Oliver Jessop, Tarka Kings, Tim Knox, Edgar Laguinia, Catherine Lampert, Todd Longstaffe-Gowan, Vanessa Nicolson, Charles Saumarez Smith, Andreas Scholl, Richard Shone, Linder Sterling, Tom Stoppard, Tom Stuart-Smith, Alison Turnbull, Edmund de Waal, Joseph Walsh, Alister Warman, Christopher Williams, Elena Williams and the staff at Hardwick Hall. India Hobson provided new photographs to illustrate the seven scenes.

On the publishing side, Zoë Waldie and Gill Coleridge of Rogers, Coleridge & White set the wheels in motion. At Particular Books, Richard Atkinson masterminded the project, and set the inspired and challenging task of writing the book backwards. Katy Banyard made sure every aspect of the production was just right. Xa Shaw Stewart was wonderfully enthusiastic and supportive during the early stages of the book. To have Donna Poppy as a copy-editor should be every writer's dream.

Victoria Hely-Hutchinson took the extraordinary pictures that so perfectly capture the character and beauty of Chatsworth, and offer a vital new perspective on a much-photographed house.

Huw Morgan art-directed and designed the book—endlessly amazing us all with both his creative vision and his meticulous attention to detail—ably assisted by Joel Antoine-Wilkinson and his colleagues at Graphic Thought Facility. Kam Tang provided the intricately riddling illuminated letters which open the book and the seven scenes.

Heartfelt thanks to Stoker and Amanda Cavendish, Duke and Duchess of Devonshire, who not only commissioned this book, but provided endless assistance and generous hospitality throughout its making; also to William Burlington, who offered both encouragement and valuable insights. Finally, thank you to my own family—to Katie and to Xanthe—for all their support and inspiration throughout.

John-Paul Stonard
May 2021

John-Paul Stonard is an art historian and writer. He was a curator of the acclaimed exhibition 'Kenneth Clark: Looking for Civilisation' at Tate Britain in 2014. He is a regular contributor to the *London Review of Books* and the *Times Literary Supplement*, and the author of *Creation: Art Since the Beginning*.

Victoria Hely-Hutchinson is a photographer and director based between London and New York. Her work has been shown internationally, including at Somerset House, the National Portrait Gallery, and the UN in Amsterdam for International Women's Day. She has been commissioned by Miu Miu, Stella McCartney, Burberry, *The Wall Street Journal Magazine*, *The New Yorker*, *Apartamento* and *Vanity Fair*.

Huw Morgan is Principal of Graphic Thought Facility, a London-based design consultancy with an international reputation for print, identity and environmental graphics, whose clients include Gagosian Gallery, Avedon Foundation, Dior, Standard Hotels, Josef and Anni Albers Foundation, Vitra and COS.

A Note on the Type

The type on the jacket and case is based on letterforms from *Regulae Trium Ordinum Literarum Typographicarum, or, The Rules of the Three Orders of Print Letters*, by Joseph Moxon, published in 1676 ('Useful for Writing Masters, Painters, Carvers, Masons, and others that are Lovers of Curiosity') of which a copy exists in the Library at Chatsworth. The text is set in ITC Galliard, a typeface designed by Matthew Carter that was released in 1978; it was based on the sixteenth-century type of the printer Robert Granjon, and its name derives from the galliard, a spirited dance of the Elizabethan Age.

First published in the
United States of America in 2022 by
Rizzoli International Publications, Inc.
300 Park Avenue South
New York, NY 10010
www.rizzoliusa.com

Originally published in 2021
by Particular Books, an imprint
of Penguin Random House UK.

Design and art direction
by Graphic Thought Facility

Jacket design by Rizzoli International Publications, Inc.

Kaleidoscopic images on pages xi–xii, 1–2, 11–12, 53–4, 63–4, 105–6, 115–16, 157–8, 167–8, 209–10, 219–20, 261–2, 271–2, 313–14, 323–4, 365–6 © Graphic Thought Facility

Illustrations on binding and pages i, 3, 55, 107, 159, 211, 263, 315 © Kam Tang

Archive photographs from
The Devonshire Collections

Moxon Regular typeface drawn by Housestyle

ISBN-13: 978-0-8478-7141-4
Library of Congress Catalog Control Number:
2021940501

2021 2022 2023 2024 / 10 9 8 7 6 5 4 3 2 1

Printed and bound in Italy by L.E.G.O. S.p.A.

Visit us online:
Facebook.com/RizzoliNewYork
Twitter: @Rizzoli_Books
Instagram.com/RizzoliBooks
Pinterest.com/RizzoliBooks
Youtube.com/user/RizzoliNY
Issuu.com/Rizzoli

Penguin Random House is committed to a sustainable future for our business, our readers and our planet. This book is made from Forest Stewardship Council® certified paper.